Business Biographies

Shaken, Not Stirred...

... With a Twist

STEPHEN TROY

iUniverse, Inc.
Bloomington

Business Biographies
Shaken, Not Stirred ... with a Twist

iUniverse books may be ordered through booksellers or by contacting:

iUniverse
1663 Liberty Drive
Bloomington, IN 47403
www.iuniverse.com
1-800-Authors (1-800-288-4677)

ISBN: 978-1-4502-8325-0 (sc)
ISBN: 978-1-4502-8326-7 (ebook)

Printed in the United States of America

iUniverse rev. date: 1/18/2011

Dedication

This book is dedicated to three women who have made invaluable contributions to my life. Each has called me a prince for different reasons over the years. If I am indeed one, behind every prince is a royal court. I would like to thank and acknowledge my royal court:

My mother, Florence Troy, who instilled in me the knowledge that I can accomplish anything I set my mind to.

My sister, Leslie McClure whose support and editing skills have saved this author from making some very embarrassing grammatical errors.

My wife, Leanne, whose love, support, and guidance each day helps me be a better and happier person.

Without them, the journey would not be as fulfilling.

...... I mustn't forget my father Arnold Troy. It was his love of history and business that inspired me in the pursuit of a business career and hobby of collecting Business History documents.

To my children, Lauren, Cortney and Chelsea.

You three girls are my greatest achievement

I hope these stories provide inspiration to you and your children's, children.

Table of Contents

1 Banking on Water:Aaron Burr   1
2 I'm from the Telephone Company, I'm Here To Help:
  Alexander Graham Bell   9
3 Fetch the Wagon, We Are Goin' Banking: A. P. Giannini 14
4 Hey, That Was My Idea! Benjamin Eisenstadt   21
5 Who Needs a Billion Dollars? Chuck Feeney   27
6 Super Size Me! Daniel Ludwig   33
7 A Fight to the Death Edwin Armstrong   38
8 Boy, Can That Face Sell Forrest Mars Sr.   45
9 You're In, You're Out, You're In, You're Out, You're Out!:
  Harry Snyder   50
10 So Much for Cars Henry Ford   57
11 Up in Smoke and Mirrors: Ivar Kreuger   62
12 Bottles You Say? Not Interested John Pemberton—
   Asa Candler—Ernest Woodruff   73
13 What a Circus! John Ringling   80
14 Special Delivery: Larry Hillblom   86
15 You Have to Give Him Credit: Lewis Tappan   91
16 Damn, Missed the Boat Again: Milton Hershey   99
17 Maybe Walking on the Moon Was Worth It:
   Philo Farnsworth   105
18 You Figure It Out: Powel Crosley Jr.   111
19 Who's Going to Be Responsible for This?:
   Robert Morris   116
20 It's Electrifying!: Samuel Insull   121
21 You Reap What You Sew: Isaac Merritt Singer   129
22 Two Tons of What?: Thomas Adams   135

23 Gentleman, Get Out of My Company!:
     William Durant   139
24 Nickel and Dimed: Frank W. Woolworth   145
25 Out in the Cold: Armand Hammer   150

Preface

As long as I can remember, I have been fascinated by business leaders and the founders of corporations. From the moment I picked up my first biography of real-estate developer William Zeckendorf, I was hooked on business. I was fifteen years old at the time. Over the next forty years, I collected and read hundreds of business biographies. These were the life stories of some of the most famous, influential, and successful businessmen and businesswomen in our country's corporate history. My journey has taken me from John Law, the creator of the Mississippi bubble in the sixteenth century, to the boys who founded Google in the twenty-first century.

In 1990, while browsing through a cryptology museum in Las Vegas, I developed a strong interest in document collecting. I set out to become a major collector of historical manuscripts and letters from famous business leaders. These pages helped me to separate fact from legend.

Over the past twenty years, I have amassed over two hundred documents from business titans. They encompass a wide variety of business endeavors. I concentrated my collection on hand-signed letters printed or written on the famous founder's company letterhead. Many of these manuscripts are now museum-framed and proudly displayed on the walls of my corporate headquarters in San Jose, California.

This book, *Business Biographies Shaken, Not Stirred ... with a Twist*, was inspired by my many years of entertaining guests with stories of the famous and infamous in the business world. I hope you'll be entertained by these tales too.

Introduction

Business Biographies Shaken, Not Stirred ... with a Twist tells the individual stories of business leaders who were, and still are, some of the most famous personalities of their time. Some names have endured through the years and still adorn their famous companies. Others have been forgotten by all but the occasional historian. What they have in common is the tremendous impact they made on the lives of people the world over. In these pages, the reader will learn of the unassuming billionaire who gave away his entire fortune during his lifetime to better the world, as well the scoundrel who stole billions from around the world. Some of the people contained in these pages are easily recognizable as famous household names. Other names may cause the reader to ask, "Who?"

In selecting these twenty-five personalities, I looked for something that happened in their lives that created a twist that people may not be aware of or that may surprise the reader. When choosing a well-known figure, I looked for a long-forgotten accomplishment that may have been overshadowed by other deeds. But each of these leaders had an impact so far-reaching that he changed or influenced the direction of a country, a city, or an industry.

The subjects have diverse backgrounds. There are the typical Horatio Alger rags-to-riches story and the unassuming youngsters who were thrust into greatness by war or politics. Others were just in the right place at the right time. Each had a twist or two along the way.

I have been asked many times if I have come to any conclusions as to why these people were successful. What traits did they have that enabled them to amass great fortunes? Why did people work and follow them and dedicate their lives to the success of their leadership? Were they the nicest people? Not really. Were they the meanest and toughest? Not always. The best-educated? No. Were they born rich? Not necessarily. Then what made it possible for these CEOs and founders to amass, in some cases, multi-billion-dollar bank accounts over their lifetimes?

There are a couple of traits they all had in common. First, each and every one of them had a sharp focus on his goals. They were almost blind to the views of others. None of them knew the meaning of the word "quit." They took defeat as just a bump in the road on the way to success. Second, they all had great partners. Each had a partner or a second-in-command who brought talents and skills that these leaders knew they themselves lacked and needed. Sometimes that meant unethical or illegal activity, and they found a "partner in crime." Most of the partners stayed in the background while the leader was the public face enjoying the spotlight.

It is my hope that this book *Business Biographies Shaken, Not Stirred* will leave the reader saying, "Really? I didn't know that!"

1   Banking on Water:
Aaron Burr

When you think of business and finance, American Revolutionary War figures don't usually come to mind. Several, however, made such an impact on financial markets that their deeds still have an impact more than two hundred years later. One such figure was Aaron Burr.

Burr is one of the most famous—some may say infamous—characters in American history. Revolutionary War officer, adventurer, state senator, and vice president under Jefferson were just a few of the many roles he played. In addition, Burr has the distinction of being the only vice president to be tried for treason, although he was acquitted.

Ironically, Burr may best be remembered as the featured answer in one of the popular "Got Milk?" television commercials of the early 2000s. Remember the scene? A radio show announcer, offering a prize, telephones a contestant at his office to ask the question, "Who killed Alexander Hamilton in a famous duel?" With a mouthful of dry cookies and the famous dueling pistol on the wall above his head, the young man—who just happened to work and be seated in the Aaron Burr museum—couldn't say "Aaron Burr" clearly enough to be understood by the radio host. Thanks to that television advertisement, the general public knows more about the famous duel with Alexander Hamilton than Burr's other remarkable accomplishments. The duel was just the culmination and climax of a very public, personal, political, and business rivalry in the lives of two extraordinary founding fathers.

In addition to being on opposite sides in politics, Burr and Hamilton butted heads over almost every issue. Their bickering spilled over into their personal and business lives as well.

Hamilton was a Federalist, and Burr was a Democratic-Republican. Like today's political party members, politicians would use any means they could to embarrass or thwart an opponent. Hamilton's closeness to our first president gave him tremendous power to block the ambitions of any who would challenge his authority or derail his policies. Burr was no exception to his attacks. When Hamilton was chosen by President Washington to be the first secretary of the treasury, Hamilton gained additional national power. He delighted in using that power against Burr, who himself was gaining enormous national popularity. If Burr tried to build popular support for a position, Hamilton responded by publishing negative attacks about Burr and spreading salacious rumors about his personal life. Burr was right in thinking that Hamilton was conspiring to destroy him both personally and financially.

History has recorded volumes about the political wrangling following the American Revolution. Not much has been devoted to the early commerce of the new republic. Even in the 1700s, business and politics went hand in hand. Everyone wanted to profit from this new young and struggling country, including Burr and Hamilton.

When it came to business, Burr favored real-estate speculation while Hamilton, with his vast financial knowledge, preferred banking. Both were trained and made their primary living as lawyers.

Hamilton, through his very powerful connections, applied for and was granted an early charter to open a new bank to promote commerce and expand our young struggling nation. His newly organized bank, the Bank of New York, opened its first office in lower Manhattan just after the British left American soil. The bank provided Hamilton with both financial and political rewards. As secretary of the treasury, he helped establish the United States Mint and the Bank of the United States to serve the government's financial needs. He controlled the new single federal currency and became a thorn in Burr's side. The Bank of New York is still active today, making it the oldest bank in the America.

Real-estate speculation, Burr's area of interest, was a common investment with post-Revolution citizens. Though Burr was a highly successful lawyer and politician, his track record in real-estate investment was mediocre at best. Some investments you might even call downright disastrous. Nevertheless, he was always on the lookout for the investment that would provide him with the money and prestige he so craved.

Burr's lavish spending drove him to look for alternative methods for financing his lifestyle. He was convinced that real-estate investments would eventually provide him with financial security. To accomplish his goals, he needed money—and lots of it—to buy land. When the famous bank robber Willie Sutton was asked why he robbed banks, his retort was, "That's where the money is." Burr clearly recognized that as well. Burr was driven by the idea of creating a bank of his own.

When Hamilton was awarded his bank charter, the Bank of New York had a virtual monopoly on banking, which prevented any other national banks from being established. That didn't stop Burr from trying. Burr lobbied hard to break the monopoly. He secured a bank charter for his own national bank in New York, only to be denied again and again by a Congress that backed his more popular and well-connected rival.

Tired of failing at a frontal assault, Burr figured out a way to go around through the back door. He found a loophole of sorts that he could exploit to his advantage in eventually establishing a national bank. It wasn't exactly a bank, but it would definitely do for the time being in raising money.

New York City was in desperate need of a fresh water supply for the southern parts of the city. There were outbreaks of yellow fever and other diseases in and around the city. Officials attributed the outbreaks to a shortage of fresh water and a lack of sanitation for the southern part of the city. The known solution was to build a pipeline from the Bronx River in the north and send water through Manhattan to the more populous southern areas. Fresh water flowed abundantly in the Bronx River, and diverting it would greatly improve the health and conditions of the residents of lower Manhattan.

Unfortunately for those citizens, this particular public-works project had been held up for years by the city for lack of funds. Burr, being a state politician serving New York City, was keenly aware of the problems associated with getting the waterworks project moving forward. The city's lack of action provided Burr with a solution to both his and the city's problems: he would build a private pipeline.

In the waterworks project, Burr found his "Trojan horse," a way to get into banking without actually opening a bank. He set in motion the creation of the Manhattan Water Company. The Manhattan Company, as it was called, would supply fresh water to the citizens of New York City.

Private ownership of a utility was not allowed in colonial America. It would take an act of Congress to give Burr the right to build an aqueduct, divert the water in the Bronx River, and sell it to the citizens of New York. He needed the help of the same Congress that had turned him down when he applied for a bank charter. More importantly, he needed the support of Alexander Hamilton. Surprisingly, Hamilton signed on, and the two bitter rivals pushed through the legislation that created the Manhattan Company, headed by Burr.

Hamilton had two motives for promoting Burr's plan. First and foremost, it would help the city of New York. Second, it would be very profitable. Hamilton insisted on one third of the stock in the newly formed company for his services, to which Burr happily agreed. Hamilton wasn't aware that Burr was working behind the scenes to blunt Hamilton's influence in the company. Burr, as the founder of the Manhattan Company, was responsible for writing the charter for the new entity. Along with the standard operating rules, Burr included some very unusual provisions in the bylaws of the utility charter that would help him to one day attain his goal of establishing a bank to compete with the Bank of New York.

Burr, without Hamilton's knowledge, included provisions in the water-company charter that allowed Burr to invest surplus funds of the Manhattan Company as he saw fit. This meant that Burr's Manhattan Company could take deposits and excess cash and loan them to credit-worthy customers, allowing it to act as a de facto bank.

Another unusual decision by Burr was the pricing of the Manhattan Company stock. Burr priced each share at fifty dollars. That seems normal by today's standards, but it was several hundred dollars a share cheaper than most of the stock that was being offered by companies seeking investors. Because the stock was priced so low, more citizens could buy into the company, thereby diluting Hamilton's influence. Should Burr want to compete head-on with the Bank of New York, Hamilton would have to find too many small stockholders to agree with him to change the charter.

There was a third unusual entry in the bylaws that would play a significant role in business history almost 150 years after the death of both Burr and Hamilton.

By no means was Burr done lobbying Congress for a change in the bank-charter laws. With much perseverance, Burr finally did succeed in getting Congress to allow him to establish a fully chartered bank. Burr's new bank, christened the Bank of Manhattan, received its charter from the government in 1799. The Bank of Manhattan was to become one of the most successful banks in the nation. Unfortunately, Burr was not able to enjoy the success.

His new access to easy money proved to be his downfall. Because of the economic roller coaster the new nation experienced in those early days, Burr was caught up in failed real-estate projects and other bad business dealings. He was forced to flee the country to escape his creditors. He did eventually return to America, where he lived under an assumed name in order to avoid his creditors. He died a ruined man in Staten Island, New York, in 1836.

The Bank of Manhattan, on the other hand, outlived its founder by almost two hundred years. The bank operated independently under the name Bank of Manhattan until 1955, when it merged with the much larger Chase Bank. Although Chase Bank was the largest bank in the world, it was Burr's much smaller Bank of Manhattan that swallowed Chase.

As it turned out, Burr had placed one more trick up his sleeve to stop Hamilton from getting control of the water company. One of the many provisions that Burr wrote into the Manhattan Company's charter prevented the Bank of Manhattan from being taken over without the unanimous consent of the stockholders. So in order for the merger to take place, the Bank of Manhattan needed to take over Chase, rather than the other way around. The new entity was called the Chase Manhattan Bank and was controlled by Chase Bank's largest stockholder, the famous Rockefeller family.

A merger in 2000 that joined Chase Manhattan Bank with J. P. Morgan Bank brought about what is known today as JPMorgan Chase. At that time, "Manhattan" was dropped from the corporate name—but not from the new bank's history or identity. After all, who would want to throw away two hundred years of banking history? Instead of casting aside the past, JPMorgan Chase found a way to embrace its 1799 founding in a unique way: not in its name, but in its corporate logo.

If you are near a Chase Bank branch or have a Chase credit card in your wallet, pull it out and look at the corporate logo. To you, it might appear to be a plain octagon. To JPMorgan Chase, it's part of a rich corporate heritage, a two-hundred-year-old symbol of its founder's dream. You might see an octagon. Aaron Burr would know it as a cross-section of wooden water pipe.

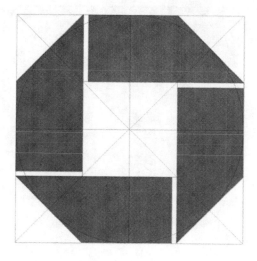

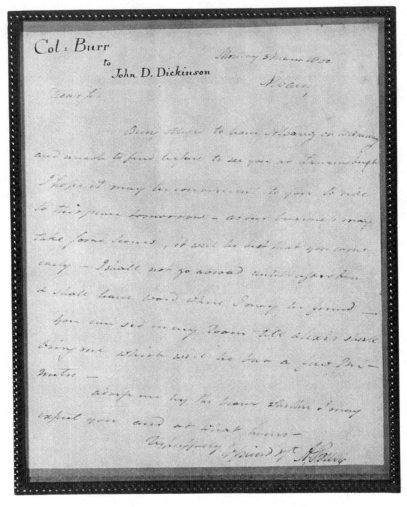

Letter to John Dickinson Signed by Aaron Burr

2 I'm from the Telephone Company, I'm Here To Help: Alexander Graham Bell

The telephone is one of the few inventions that actually changed the course of history. As with many great innovations, several people claimed to be the first and true creators of the device that sent voice over wires. The list of those who claimed to have invented the telephone is extensive, including such names as Thomas Edison, Elisha Gray, Innocenzo Manzetti, Johann Reis, and of course, Alexander Graham Bell.

As we know, the full credit has been given to Bell, since he is the one who filed the first patent. But did he actually invent the telephone? With so many people staking a claim to that accomplishment, it was only natural that one of these men would challenge Bell's patent.

The first challenge came from Elisha Gray. Gray was not only an early inventor of the telephone, but he was also the first to get to the patent office with an application. Gray's problem was that he didn't insist that the clerk immediately file the application the moment he arrived. Unfortunately for Gray, the application was in a basket at the patent office at the time Bell's lawyer arrived and had the clerk file his papers while he waited. Thus, Gray's earlier application was actually logged in later.

The invention of the telephone altered life as we know it, and a simple lack of urgency on Gray's part changed the fortunes of both men and their place in history. Bell went on to become a celebrated and very wealthy inventor. He went down in history for discovering the phone that changed the world.

It might be easy to say that Elisha Gray's mistake made him fade into the background a ruined man, but that is just not the case. Elisha Gray went on to file many more patents. His most famous was the 1888 patent for the telautograph, a machine that could transmit handwritten pages over the phone lines to be received by a machine at the other end. One hundred years later, Gray's machine was renamed the fax machine.

Bell's genius at inventing is undisputed. His skill and success in business, on the other hand, might be attributed to a great deal of luck. Not only was Bell awarded the patent for the telephone ahead of Gray's patent, which arrived at the patent office several hours before, but he was also the recipient of one of the most famous rejections in business history.

After winning his patent lawsuit with Gray, Bell wanted to get back to his laboratory to continue his experiments and solve problems through inventions. Bell was not interested in running a company, manufacturing and selling telephones. He was a researcher and an inventor who wanted to continue his work in the lab. With the patent dispute trial behind him, he offered his telephone patents to the Western Union Company. The asking price was $100,000, an amount that the president of Western Union, William Orton, found outrageous. He thought it much too much to pay for "nothing more than a toy."

Only two years later, William Orton would regret his words. He told a friend that if he could get his hands on the telephone patent for $25 million, it would be a bargain. By this time, Bell was a millionaire many times over from the royalties he was receiving from licensed manufacturers.

The royalties and sales of the telephone allowed Bell to get back into his laboratory and continue his quest for other great innovations. During that period, Bell invented, or co-invented, a slew of products for which he received patents. Some were for improvements to the telephone, while others were totally unrelated, including the hydrofoil boat, alternative fuels, a machine to detect icebergs, and a method for putting magnetic data on tape. His magnetic-data research would later lead to the creation of the tape recorder, floppy disks, and hard drives that ushered in the computer age. Bell is also credited with building the first working metal detector.

Bell's metal detector was the second of his inventions that changed the course of history. While the telephone changed how people communicated and made a big world smaller, the metal detector, or should we say its lack of a working metal detector, changed the political landscape of the United States in a very unusual way. Bell rushed the research and development of the metal detector not to win a race to the patent office, but to save a life.

Bell's inspiration came on July 2, 1881. He spent most of his time before bed reading and looking for areas of interest and problems that needed solutions. It was on one such occasion that he read on the front page of the newspaper that the president of the United States, James Garfield, had been shot by an assassin outside the Sixth Street train station in Washington, DC. The assassin, Charles Guiteau, angry that Garfield's administration would not appoint him to a civil-service job, shot Garfield as the president was on his way to deliver a speech at Williams College, Garfield's alma mater. It is speculated that Guiteau felt he would get better treatment if Garfield's successor, Chester A. Arthur, were president.

Garfield was not killed during the attack. One bullet grazed his arm, and the attending doctors speculated that the second bullet lodged itself somewhere near Garfield's spine. Unfortunately for Garfield, the doctors could not locate the exact spot where the bullet stopped. Doctors probed and prodded with little success. Several of the doctors made the situation worse by inserting their fingers in the wound. One of them even punctured the president's liver.

When Garfield was shot, Bell was working on an idea for a device that could detect metal underground. When he read about the assassination attempt on the president, Bell was sure he could help. To save the president, Bell hastily hooked his crude metal detector to an amplifier from one of his telephones to provide an audio detection. After several experiments in his laboratory, he was confident the machine would work well enough to find the metal bullet lodged in the president's back. With his newly developed makeshift metal detector, Bell headed to Washington, DC, to offer his services to the president.

The Secret Service was very skeptical of Bell and his device. It took some time before Bell was able to convince them to allow him and his equipment to approach the ailing president. When they all finally agreed, Bell's first request was that Garfield be moved onto the floor for the experiment. Not surprisingly, the Secret Service did not grant that request, stating that the president couldn't be moved, and Bell could only use the contraption while Garfield was in his bed.

At first, the detector Bell had used successfully in his laboratory didn't work on Garfield. Bell was getting readings that were all over the place. Bell figured the electronics may have been damaged during his travels to Washington. Not seeing success, the Secret Service and the attending doctors quickly lost patience and asked Bell to leave and take his contraption with him. However, Bell was not discouraged. He went back to his hotel room and worked through the night recalibrating his invention. By morning, his metal detector was working flawlessly.

Looking to be vindicated, Bell headed back to see President Garfield. He had to convince an even more skeptical Secret Service to let him try again. Garfield was definitely getting worse, so what was the harm? The president's aides and doctors were ready to try just about anything. Bell again requested that the president be moved to the floor. Again, the Secret Service said no. He would have to use his gadget on Garfield while the president was lying in bed. Bell turned on the power and went over the body, looking for the distinctive rapid sound that would indicate the location of the bullet that had come to rest in Garfield's back. Unfortunately for Garfield, the machine again went haywire and could not find the bullet.

Bell left Garfield's bedside very disappointed, retreating back to his hotel to work on his metal detector once more, still not locating the problem. While Bell pondered what went wrong and why he couldn't locate the ill-fated bullet, President Garfield passed away on Sept, 19, 1881, two-and-a-half months after he was shot.

It wasn't until after Garfield's death that Bell figured out what went wrong in the hotel room those two agonizing days that the metal detector did not work. President Garfield had been laying on another new invention of the day: the metal spring mattress. Bell's metal detector was reading the large springs under the mattress, not the bullet. If Garfield had been moved to the floor as Bell requested, the president might have survived.

With the death of President James Garfield, Chester A. Arthur became the president of the United States. Arthur and Garfield had never been friends. They didn't see eye to eye politically. Arthur had been chosen to run with Garfield as a political favor to the Stalwarts (a Republican faction) in an effort to assure their votes. The Stalwarts were a part of the Republican Party that was against a civil-service merit system. With the death of Garfield, the Stalwarts were sure they now had the right man as president.

However, much to their chagrin, after Garfield's passing, Chester A. Arthur—a man whose whole political career had been based on favoritism—made a 180-degree turn. He pushed through and got passed the first civil-service act in the United States, which effectively eliminated the exchange of government jobs for political favors.

3   Fetch the Wagon, We Are Goin' Banking: A. P. Giannini

If you make a list of the ten most influential people in the history of finance, A. P. Giannini would have to be on that list. Yet Giannini wasn't born into a banking family, and he didn't have a background in finance.

Giannini was born in San Jose, California, in 1870. The boardinghouse that once stood on that site has now been demolished to make way for a three-story parking garage in the middle of downtown. The site is commemorated with a bronze plaque that pays tribute to A. P. Giannini, one of San Jose's most famous residents.

Growing up in an Italian immigrant farming family, Giannini was like most Italian immigrants living in America. His family was in the agricultural business, which was a long way from Wall Street or even the financial district of San Francisco.

When Giannini was seven years old, he watched as his father was shot while trying to collect a ten-dollar debt. This caused Giannini to work that much harder to help support his family. His mother remarried a few years after his father died.

At age fourteen, Giannini dropped out of school to join his stepfather in the produce business. Giannini immediately earned a reputation for being trustworthy and honest. Farmers always

14

knew they could get a fair deal with him, and he always provided the buyers of his goods with the best and freshest produce, no matter what time of day the purchase took place.

After a few years, Giannini was able to buy into his stepfather's produce business as a full partner. He continued his reputation for fair and honest business dealings.

By his thirty-first birthday, after being in the produce business for eighteen years, Giannini decided to sell his half of the business to the employees and retire. Fate would later take him out of retirement and thrust him into banking history.

When Giannini's father-in-law died unexpectedly, he inherited stock and a seat on the board of the Bank of Columbus in San Francisco's North Beach District. At the time, most banks in the country only loaned money to large businesses and wealthy individuals. The middle class and small-business owners had no access to bank capital.

Giannini tried at every board meeting to get the bank to offer loans to the "little fellow," the small shopkeepers and hard-working immigrants who worked in the San Francisco Bay area. The board wanted nothing to do with them. Board member after board member reminded him that the bank loaned money to those with the means and the ability to pay back loans. Banks did not loan money to people who clearly would be at risk of not repaying the loan.

Giannini was incensed. He knew the little guys. Most of them were credit-worthy people who paid their bills. After being turned down again and again, Giannini finally left the board and marched into his attorney's office to find out what he needed to do in order to open a bank.

With help from his lawyer and $150,000 in capital that he raised from his stepfather and a few friends, Giannini succeeded in opening the Bank of Italy. The bank was housed in a rented saloon in North Beach, directly across the street from the bank where he was once a director, the Columbus Savings and Loan. He even hired the bartender as an assistant teller. Focusing on the "little guy," Giannini steadily built deposits and loans. These middle-class workers and the many different types of immigrants that called the Bay Area home became stockholders in this new bank. With the support of the common man and a steady supply of money flowing into the bank, Giannini traveled the state, opening branches and buying small banks to turn them into branches of the Bank of Italy.

Giannini's big break came two years after he opened the bank. On the morning of April 16, 1906, Giannini was rocked out of bed by a giant earthquake. After he made sure his family was safe, he hitched a team of horses to a vegetable wagon and traveled into North Beach. He wanted to get there ahead of the fires so as to save his depositors' money.

Giannini transferred the gold and currency from the vault to his wagon. He hid the money under the produce to protect it from looters. He then successfully traveled the eighteen miles back to his home in San Mateo, a rural outpost of the city.

A few days later, when the fires died down, he packed up the vegetable wagon and headed back into the city. The Bank of Italy was in smoldering ruins, as were the bank buildings of all of his competitors. The full bank vaults belonging to his competitors were standing in the middle of the charred sites. The contents were destroyed, and the vaults were still red hot. Only the Bank of Italy's vault had been emptied, thanks to the quick thinking and fast action of its founder.

The bankers agreed not to re-open their doors until the full extent of the disaster was assessed—all, that is, except Giannini. He brought his wagon back to the rubble where the bank had been. He laid a large plank of wood over two barrels and announced that he was open for business. With all of the bank documents burned in the fire, Giannini made loans based on signatures and a handshake. He loaned money to anyone who wanted to rebuild. Years later, he took great pride in the fact that every one of those loans had been paid back in full. Giannini's faith in his borrowers and his competitor's inability to make loans gave the Bank of Italy a virtual monopoly.

Giannini created many of the services that we take for granted today. Home mortgages, car loans, and installment loans were all innovations of Giannini's Bank of Italy.

Giannini worked round the clock. He worked harder than any of his fellow bankers. He walked the streets, knocked on doors, and explained to anyone who would listen what services his bank offered. He did everything to beat the competition.

At one point, while traveling to the home of a prospective borrower, Giannini spotted a rival banker on the same route. Giannini cut through the woods, dismounted from his horse, and swam through a pond. He arrived dripping wet at the home of the astonished depositor.

Giannini's reputation spread throughout California. To further his goal as the bank for the "little guy," he championed branch banking. After the San Francisco earthquake, Giannini believed his bank needed to be in more geographic regions, not dependent on one area. Fellow bankers were not happy that he opened branches in their towns. His largest competitors eventually complained to the banking authorities and tried to stop the growth.

His competitors tried to block Giannini's goal of nationwide branch banking, and in some cases they succeeded. Giannini fought back by starting a holding company to get around the prohibition. Giannini found himself at odds with the banking regulators over his stand on branch banking. The tensions escalated when he entered the lucrative Los Angeles market. But by that time, his bank was not only attracting the little guy but also the wealthy.

In 1928, looking for more growth, Giannini bought two banks, including the third largest bank in the city, Bank of America Los Angeles. The purchase of Bank of America Los Angeles created a true statewide bank-branch system.

Giannini was on his way to creating the first nationwide bank. He formed a holding company, Bancitaly, in New York to purchase the East River Bank in Brooklyn. Although East River Bank was a small New York bank with a mere $3.5 million in assets, Giannini was able to create the third largest bank in New York. He purchased the stock of the very old and well-respected original Bank of America in New York from its squabbling stockholders. Then he merged East River with his new acquisition. It was the purchase of Bank of America in New York that was eventually the impetus for Giannini to merge the Bank of Italy with Bank of America California. He changed the corporate name to Bank of America National Trust and Savings Association.

Giannini's willingness to enter markets that other bankers shunned allowed him to finance some of the greatest entrepreneurs and projects of the twentieth century.

Bank of America provided David Packard and Bill Hewlett with a loan for their famous "garage" company, known today simply as HP. He gave Walt Disney the money to fulfill his dream of creating the first feature-length animated movie, *Snow White and the Seven Dwarves*. Giannini signed off on loans to the movie industry and the emerging Napa wine industry. He helped finance Anaheim's Disneyland and the construction of the famous Golden Gate Bridge.

But all was not easy for Giannini. He was constantly at battle with federal regulators who were acting on behalf of angry competitors. He even battled with the powerful Wall Street banker J. P. Morgan.

In 1930, Giannini again decided to retire. He believed the bank was in good hands with his handpicked successor and left California to travel. When he received word in 1931 that the board had betrayed his vision and was selling his branches, thereby playing into the hands of wealthy Wall Street bankers, he returned to California. But he was forced to resign from the board.

With the sale of the New York Bank of America holdings, which he had worked so hard to put together, Giannini declared war on the board. He organized a group of unhappy shareholders and came out of retirement to wage a proxy battle to regain control of the bank. By 1932, Giannini, supported by an overwhelming three-to-one majority of Bank of America shareholders, won back control of his beloved Bank of America. The *San Francisco Chronicle* said the outcome was "the greatest Wall Street defeat of all times."

Giannini's love for Bank of America and his desire to help the little guy were not motivated by money. The truth was, Giannini owned very little of his own bank. He ran the bank for the people, not for personal gain. Giannini could have easily been a millionaire many times over. In fact, he did his best *not* to have millions. He believed that if he were rich, it would separate him from the people he wanted to serve.

When the board of Bank of America voted a year later to give him a surprise $1.5 million bonus, he refused to take it. He set up a foundation and promptly gave the money to the University of California. He continued this practice while his net worth rose to the millionaire level.

After guiding the bank through the Great Depression and the war years, Giannini decided to retire from Bank of America again. In 1945, at the age of 74, he left his beloved bank. Frustrated with federal regulation that prevented him from creating a true nationwide branch bank, he felt the most he could do at Bank of America was to be "a barking watchdog."

Giannini managed to avoid what he called the "money itch." Upon his death, his total estate was valued at just under $500,000, which was by his own choice. He owned very little Bank of America stock at the time of his death, just under a quarter of one percent. In his words, "No man actually owns a fortune, it owns him …."

Bancitaly Corporation

CAPITAL AND SURPLUS
TWENTY-SIX MILLION DOLLARS

San Francisco, California.

December 7, 1925.

Gr.Uff. Lionello Perera,
38 West 83rd Street,
New York City, N.Y.

My dear Commendatore:

While it may be possible that I shall come out East between now and Christmas, my family is urging me not to do so.

I am, therefore, trying to do all possible to defer my trip until after Christmas, unless absolutely necessary.

I have some very important things to look after at Washington, which will require my personal attention and it will only be these matters that will bring me on there sooner. However, I am planning to surely be there along about the end of the year or first of January, at which time I shall get in touch with you in regard to the matter which we have had under consideration.

Anticipating the pleasure of seeing you soon, and wishing you and yours a Merry Christmas and a Happy and Prosperous New Year, I remain,

Yours very sincerely,

A. Giannini,
President.

APG:ALB

A.P. Giannini signed document on Bancitaly Corporation stationary. Bank of Italy officially changed its name to Bank of America in 1930. Bancitaly Corporation was a holding company.

4 Hey, That Was My Idea!
Benjamin Eisenstadt

Benjamin Eisenstadt graduated first in his class with a law degree from St. John's University. Unfortunately for him, the year was 1929, and it was the start of the Great Depression. Law firms were laying people off, not hiring them. Undaunted and unable to find a firm to join, Eisenstadt opened his own practice and waited for clients. He waited and waited and waited, but there were few to be found.

In need of a steady income and wanting to help his wife's ailing father, he took over and ran his father-in law's cafeteria in Flatbush, New York. He worked as a counterman. It was there he found his first big client. There was much talk at the courthouse about this young, bright, energetic lawyer who was "defending criminals while serving up coffee, apple pie, and legal advice between court appearances".

The cafeteria turned out to be the best thing that could have happened to Ben. It allowed him to continue the practice of law while providing a steady income. It also had another surprising effect on his life. The cafeteria became a hangout for the notorious Murder Inc. gang, and Ben was only too eager to offer his services to the gang members when they were arrested. Ben overheard many of the conversations of the accused gang members while working at the counter. He was quick to give advice. It was during one of these conversations that Ben overheard a man who feared being arrested ask a detective if he would need a lawyer. Like Superman, Ben stripped off his linen jacket, donned a dark fedora, and responded, "Sure you will, and I am the lawyer who will defend you."

Still, Ben didn't have enough cases to keep the family going. The cafeteria business took up most of Ben's time. Before long, Ben was running the operation full time. So he decided that if he was going to be in the cafeteria business full-time, he needed to think big.

The Flatbush Cafeteria was doing well, but it was just too small to support a growing family. Ben decided the best course of action was to sell the original cafeteria and build a larger one. When the new and larger cafeteria was established, he would sell that and build another even larger one and so on. Each one he built, he sold, only to build a bigger one, the whole time scrimping and saving. Neither he nor his wife, Betty, spent any money on themselves. It was the middle of the Depression, and every dollar was hard to come by.

Ben and Betty didn't know it at the time, but it was a large cafeteria on Cumberland Street in Brooklyn, across from the Navy Pier, that would change their lives. The year was 1940, and the country was just coming out of the Depression. There were rumblings about America entering the war against Germany. The Navy Pier was quiet after World War I, but it was starting to get busier as the war in Europe escalated. Ben and Betty saw an opportunity. They decided to buy the Cumberland Cafeteria from its present owner and make a go of it.

Less than a year after Ben and Betty purchased the Cumberland Cafeteria, the Japanese attacked Pearl Harbor. When Ben came to work on the day following the Pearl Harbor attack, there were a thousand men standing in line at the Navy shipyard waiting to enlist. In the blink of an eye, the world had changed, and with it, the fortunes of Ben and Betty Eisenstadt.

The war years proved very prosperous for Ben and Betty. Unfortunately, when the war ended, the good times stopped, too. In 1945, the pier was all but deserted. The tables at the Cumberland Cafeteria were empty. Ben tried to sell the diner. However, when the only prospective buyer realized that the sale price was based on the old war numbers and not the new reality of the empty pier, he pulled out of the sale. Against Betty's objections, Ben returned the deposit and ripped up the contract. Ben had survived the Depression and a world war. He would get through this next chapter honorably, too.

With very few customers coming into the cafeteria, Ben decided it was time to close for good. He had a plan for the future and working behind a counter was not it.

When Ben originally purchased the cafeteria, he also bought the building that went with it. With the economy booming after the war, he decided to become a manufacturer. He ripped out the counters and the booths and decided to turn the old cafeteria into a factory. Ben was going to make tea bags.

Tea bags, which were nothing more than a sack filled with tea, were first invented in 1903. By 1944, the more modern rectangular bag was invented, and tea bags were rising in popularity. Ben and Betty ordered a tea-bagging machine from a supply company in Massachusetts. They hung a new hand-painted sign over the old cafeteria sign and announced that the new Cumberland Packing Company was open for business.

The Cumberland Packing Company was anything but a success. Ben crawled all over the tea-bag machine kicking and cursing it to keep it running. As the tea bags came out of the machine, his wife, Betty, and his mother-in-law packed them into small boxes and then into bigger boxes ready to ship to customers. But unfortunately, they had no customers. The world by this time was awash in tea bags. The bills rolled in, but no tea bags rolled out.

With the business failing, Ben and Betty went to lunch to discuss their options. They talked about each tea bag as if it was an unwanted child and pondered how to increase sales. As fate would have it, while trying to pour sugar in her coffee, Betty noticed that the large glass jar with the metal spout that held the sugar was clogged. The sugar was dry, lumpy, and crystallized. It wouldn't pour through the spout. No matter how hard she bumped, knocked, or shook the jar, nothing came out. It was reminiscent of the sugar containers at the Cumberland Cafeteria. Betty had a heck of a time keeping the sugar dry because of the moist salt air at the pier.

Betty yelled out *"Why not pack sugar?!"* Ben got it immediately. Of course—use the tea-bag machine to pack individual personal servings of sugar that were clean, sanitary, dry, and disposable. The tea-bag machine was perfect. What difference did it make if the machine put tea in a bag or sugar? There was nothing on the market like it.

Ben worked on the tea-bag machine for weeks to modify it to handle sugar and paper packets. When he finally had it all worked out, he was ready to take on customers. His first call was to the Domino Sugar refinery just across the river in lower Manhattan.

Domino, owned by the American Sugar Company, could trace its roots back to the founding families of New York. Ben thought if he could get the order to pack Domino's sugar packets, that would be the only customer he needed.

After his presentation to the heads of Domino, they seemed very interested and promised to get back to him quickly. One week went by, then two, then three. Finally, after a month, Ben got through to the bosses at Domino's. They told him that his idea and design was very clever. It was so clever, in fact, that they had already built a machine of their own for the sugar packets and wouldn't need his services.

Never again would he be so naïve as to show anyone his ideas without a patent. Ben had no choice but to move on. He went through New York meeting with smaller refiners and customers, convincing them to buy their individual personal sugar packets from Cumberland. By 1950, Ben had developed a prosperous business selling individually packaged sugar, duck sauce, perfume, and even subway tokens.

Ben's company was making over a $100,000 a year. He took only enough money to support his family modestly and put everything else back into the factory. In 1956, executives from a pharmaceutical company approached Ben and his son, Marvin, who had been working in the factory after college. They asked if the Cumberland Packing Company could come up with a fake sugar that could be put into individual packages to be used in hospitals and nursing homes. At the time, artificial sweetener only came in pill or liquid form. Ben and Marvin didn't know it then, but they were about to enter into "a plot to overthrow sugar," which has been a staple of the Western diet for five hundred years.

Ben hired a chemist. The three of them worked on a sugar substitute that would have the look, taste, and feel of sugar. Saccharin was the natural starting point. The problem was that saccharin, the most common dietary sweetener, when used without additives, had a nasty aftertaste. If they were to find a sweetener with the look, feel, and taste of sugar, they were going to have to find a way to bulk up the saccharin and mask the aftertaste. Ben was pulling his hair out. He was testing coffee samples using different additives and was coming up with nothing. It was Marvin who found the answer in a cookbook: lactose. Lactose bulked up foods and leached out taste.

With their formula complete, Ben and Marvin went back to the pharmaceutical company that originally gave them the project. The executives hardly even remembered the Eisenstadts coming to see them. When Ben tried to convince the men to taste coffee with his sugar substitute, they just weren't interested. Ben and Marvin had worked so hard, they had succeeded in creating a sugar substitute that tasted like sugar with no aftertaste, and no one cared. Ben and Marvin left fuming.

Not wanting to let all their work go to waste, they decided to package the product themselves and create a brand. Ben chose pink for the packaging so it would stand out among the white sugar packets that were being served to diners. The name was Ben's idea. He took the name from the title of a Tennyson poem that was set to song. Not about to make the same mistake twice, Ben applied for and received a use patent for his sugar substitute. The Cumberland Packing Company also received the one millionth service mark registration for the new product's name, "Sweet'N Low."

Sweet'N Low is now served around the world. It is still being manufactured in the Cumberland Cafeteria on Cumberland Street in Brooklyn, New York. Today, the cafeteria has taken over the rest of the warehouse space around it and expanded to a full city block. Ben did not live long enough to see the Domino Sugar refinery close its doors in Manhattan. It was an event he surely would have been happy to see.

5 Who Needs a Billion Dollars?
Chuck Feeney

You've probably never heard of him, but Chuck Feeney is undoubtedly one of the most successful entrepreneurs of all time. Yes, that is a very bold statement. But he was a master of most everything: master of his craft, master of timing, and master of finding ways to better mankind. Very bold statements all.

Chuck Feeney grew up in New Jersey during the Depression. Kicking back for a while after high school, Chuck decided to join the air force. Trained as a radio operator, he was sent to Japan just after the war ended. After serving his tour of duty, Chuck—like many other veterans—decided to take advantage of the new GI Bill to pay for college. Trying to decide on a career, he happened upon the hospitality industry. He realized it was really all about taking care of people. He knew he would be good at it. He researched colleges that provided an education in hospitality and decided on Cornell University.

His GI Bill only provided $110 a month while he was in school. After tuition, that didn't leave much to live on. To make extra money, Chuck started a sandwich business. He made and delivered sandwiches on campus. With an eye toward cost, he made a decent product and delivered the sandwiches after hours to dorms and fraternity houses. He sold sandwiches into the night and early morning. The students were always happy to see Chuck, not only for his late-night snacks but also for his outgoing personality.

College went by quickly. Chuck graduated with a degree in hospitality management. Although the sandwich business was successful, Chuck didn't see a future in it. For Chuck, it was never about the money. It was the excitement of creating something, making deals, and making things happen.

Soon after college, Chuck headed to Europe. It was there that he met an Englishman by the name of Bob Edmunds. Edmunds was looking for an American to help him sell liquor to servicemen on navy ships that were coming into ports around Europe. Edmunds explained to Chuck that service personnel were not able to drink on ships. They were, however, able to buy five bottles of spirits, duty free, and bring them home as unaccompanied luggage. This was a 50 percent savings to the servicemen. Chuck liked the idea and signed on.

While waiting for a ship in Barcelona, Chuck thumbed through his Cornell directory and saw that a fellow graduate, Bob Miller, was working at the Ritz Hotel in Barcelona. He decided to pay Bob a visit, and the two of them hit it off. Chuck told Bob about the liquor idea, and Bob was hooked. Chuck suggested they form a partnership to cover Europe. The new enterprise was to be called Tourist International.

Chuck and Bob chased the US Sixth Fleet all around Europe. Before long, they were shipping thousands of duty-free cases of liquor back home to American soldiers and sailors. When a sailor offhandedly asked if they sold cars duty-free back to the states, they suddenly found themselves in the car business. They formed a new company, Cars International, to sell European cars at a tremendous savings to returning servicemen. They were well on their way to becoming millionaires.

Always looking for new ways to sell liquor, Chuck came across a beautiful full-color catalog that offered perfume, watches, scarves, and numerous other duty-free items. Chuck thought this was a brilliant idea and flew to the headquarters in Switzerland to convince the owners to insert his liquor flyers in the catalogs. When he got to the office, he was shocked to find the president, Henry Adler, cleaning out his desk. Duty Free Shoppers, as the company was called, was shutting down because of poor sales. Chuck was sure the idea was a winner and only lacked his creative marketing talents. Before long, Chuck and Bob were the new owners of the Duty Free Shoppers catalog business—along with their new junior partner, Henry Adler.

Heavy competition forced the partners to expand globally. Bob took Asia, and Chuck, along with their new partner, stayed in Europe. The company's big break came when Bob heard of an opportunity in Honolulu, Hawaii. The new airport commission was looking for a duty-free shop to open at its new terminal. The partners applied for and won a concession to open their first duty-free store, which they called Tourist International Sales. It was the right time and the right place. Japan, which was just recovering from the war, was starting to show life. The government was lifting restrictions on travel for its citizens. It was also lifting restrictions on how much money they could take out of the country. As these restrictions were lifted, the Japanese flooded into Hawaii. Tourist International Sales not only benefited from the influx of Japanese tourists, but also from the Japanese cultural tradition of bringing back gifts for family, friends, and co-workers. In a short time, Tourist International Sales hired a dozen very attractive salesgirls, all with the ability to speak Japanese. These girls would line up in front of the store to attract customers every time a plane landed from Japan. The same scenario was repeated in Hong Kong. The traffic there grew so great at the airport store that Bob had to open a second store in downtown Hong Kong to capture the thousands of tourists who came in each day. Bob resorted to paying tour guides a commission on sales if they drove their tour groups to the store before they checked into their hotels.

The company grew and profits flowed. Each year, the partners—who now numbered four—met in secret to divide up the profits. And the profits were impressive. Tens of millions of dollars in checks were distributed to each partner. Over the years, hundreds of millions were paid to the partners. Chuck used most of his money to invest in new business opportunities. He built hotels, bought a chain of retail stores, and invested wisely in other moneymaking endeavors. Chuck hardly spent a dollar on himself. He didn't buy fancy cars, hire servants, or live a lavish lifestyle. He took the bus, flew coach, lived in small apartments, and ate in small, unimpressive restaurants that made good sandwiches. He was the same ordinary guy who grew up in New Jersey during the Depression.

It wasn't long before Chuck and his partners were billionaires. It was time for Chuck's next venture. He had spent years making money, and now it was time to spend it. Chuck and his wife landed in the Bahamas on November 23, 1984, for an historic event. Chuck was going to give away all of his money. His wife and kids would be cared for, and he would keep less than $5 million for himself. The rest of his billions would go into a nonprofit charitable trust—a trust that was independent and irreversible.

Chuck sought a leader for the trust who would be respected and beyond reproach. Chuck would then find worthy causes to be the recipients of his billions of dollars. He would give away the money the same way he made it, shrewdly and wisely, while getting results.

And so Atlantic Philanthropies, registered in the Bahamas, became one of the richest charitable trusts in the world. No one had ever heard of it. It was a secret, and that's how Chuck liked it. The trust was made up of a combination of stock, cash, and real estate. Chuck started to learn a new business—the business of giving away money to make a difference. Since Chuck made his money secretly, he was determined to give it away secretly. Dressed casually and looking nothing like the successful billionaire he was (or used to be), Chuck asked questions of a charity's director to try to ascertain whether they were worthy and responsible enough to solve problems if the money was available. If a charity passed the test, he casually mentioned he might know a friend who could help.

It wouldn't be long, then, before someone from Atlantic Philanthropies would show up and offer the money—big money, money that would make a difference. The only requirement was that the recipient couldn't ask where the money came from. If a director tried to find that out, the money would be cut off. This cloak-and-dagger operation went on for years.

Over the years, Chuck managed to give away billions of dollars without a soul knowing about it. His billions went toward changing the lives of people around the world, creating new buildings for Cornell University, hospitals in Vietnam, and a higher-education system in Australia. He even funded an organization that was the catalyst for ending the bloody IRA war in Ireland. What many governments weren't able to do, Chuck accomplished.

Chuck's timing was always his best business asset. Atlantic needed money for new causes. He felt the time was right to sell Atlantic's large block of stock in the retail empire he had created. It was worth billions. He convinced the partners to send out requests for offers for the entire company—lock, stock, and barrel. The offers back were impressive. The winner, LVMH Möet Hennessy Louis Vuitton, offered $4.2 billion. Atlantic would receive over three billion in tax-free proceeds if the sale went through. Chuck was ready. Unfortunately, his original partner, Bob Miller, was not. Bob loved the business. He also loved the hundreds of millions in profits that went along with it. He decided to sue Chuck to stop the sale. Chuck knew that a lawsuit would eventually open the company's records to the public. The transfer of his stock to Atlantic was sure to get out. Before he was exposed by the courts, Chuck decided it was time to come clean and tell all the recipients that their billions had once been his billions. He then had Atlantic send out a press release giving the details. Controlling the publicity was his best choice.

The retail stores and all of the other businesses he had accumulated over time were eventually sold to LVMH for $4.2

billion. Bob stayed on with the stores and continues to live the life of a king. He has been knighted by the queen. His daughter was married off to a prince, and he travels the world on a magnificent yacht. Sadly, Bob and Chuck don't speak anymore. Bob is still bitter about how his "baby" was sold out from under him.

Chuck, for his part, said a sad goodbye to his employees by way of thank-you checks from his personal account. Employees weren't expecting the checks for thousands of dollars that showed up in their mailboxes shortly after the sale closed. Chuck now lives happily in a small apartment in San Francisco with his second wife. He walks or takes the bus everywhere he goes. He still travels the world, flying coach on commercial airlines. Each year, he hops from one place to another, circling the globe, looking for ways to give away an additional $4 billion. His plan is to see that every dime has been spent on worthy projects by 2016.

The retail empire he and his partners started is still in airports around the world. DFS, or Duty Free Shops, is now a part of LVMH and doing well.

6 Super Size Me!
Daniel Ludwig

Not many people can claim to have a net worth in excess of a billion dollars. Fewer still have been named the richest person in the world by *Forbes* magazine. Since *Forbes* has kept track of such wealth, only a handful of people have been named the number-one richest person in the world. In 1982, *Forbes* gave that title to Daniel Ludwig.

Daniel Ludwig started his career in his hometown of South Haven, Michigan, located on the banks of Lake Michigan. It was there that he became interested in ships and shipping. By the age of nineteen, he felt he had enough knowledge and experience to start his own shipping company. With a $5,000 loan from his father and a handful of contacts, Daniel purchased an old steamer. He personally converted it into a barge for cargo. It was not long until he received the first of what were to be several contracts to ship molasses to ports surrounding Lake Michigan.

With his initial success in the shipping business, Ludwig looked to expand his operation into shipping other products. At the time, the United States was beginning to come out of the Depression of the 1930s. Ludwig had a feeling there would be a big demand for oil going forward. Turns out, he was right. The problem, however, was that in order to capitalize on the growing demand for oil, Ludwig needed tankers. And in order to purchase tankers, he needed financial capital.

Surprisingly, though, even without a single tanker that could ship oil, Ludwig was getting orders for charters. He just didn't have a way to move the oil without tanker financing. Finally, he hit upon a unique financing idea. Why not take the firm shipping contracts that he had in hand and borrow from a bank or insurance company? He could use the bank money to fund the building of the fleet.

Because Ludwig had virtually no experience in shipping oil, and he had very few assets, the banks in Michigan were not interested in loaning money to a small shipping company with what seemed to be only pipe dreams. He decided to move his operation to the finance center of the country, New York City.

New York was home to hundreds of banks from countries all over the world. These banks were looking to finance growing businesses. Ludwig was sure he could interest a banker in his shipping operation. He rented a small office in the city and went door to door to pitch his idea for building an oil-tanker fleet. Using a windowsill as his desk, he called New York bankers to set up appointments. Within a year, Ludwig found a bank to fund him. It was one of the largest banks in the world— Chase Manhattan Bank, whose largest stockholder and chief executive was very familiar with the oil business. After all, David Rockefeller's grandfather had founded the Standard Oil Company seventy-five years earlier.

Ludwig put his contracts up as collateral. That allowed him to borrow the money needed to build his fleet of ships. Ludwig was then able to own the ships without putting one penny of his own money into the project. The Rockefellers later became customers of Ludwig's expanded company.

By the early 1940s, Daniel Ludwig was successful enough to build his own shipyard in Virginia. He began experimenting with new and less expensive ways to build ships. Ludwig's shipyard revolutionized the shipbuilding industry when he developed a new method for welding the tankers instead of riveting them. The unusually fast speed with which Ludwig built tankers caught the eye of the US military, which was in urgent need of ships for the upcoming war effort.

Ludwig managed to land a nice contract, with extremely favorable terms, to build tankers for the US government. The agreement with the government called for the military to pay for the building of the ships and then give the tankers back to Ludwig, at no cost, after the war.

Receiving all the government ships back after the war gave Ludwig a huge a head start over the competition. The demand for oil skyrocketed after the war. Ludwig was on his way toward amassing a substantial fortune.

By 1950, Ludwig had expanded his shipbuilding operation overseas to Japan. He was able to lease, at bargain prices, the Kure naval shipyard from the Japanese government. With this large shipyard and an inexpensive labor force, Ludwig was able to build bigger and bigger ships. By 1956, when the Suez Canal was closed, the need for large ships to transport items over longer distances was even greater. Ludwig was already ahead of his competitors. He was ready to launch the largest oil carriers the world had ever seen. These ships are now known as supertankers.

Ludwig's success continued, and so did the money. But he didn't flaunt it. Ludwig still worked in a small office, although he did have a real desk. He preferred to walk to work alone. He was regularly seen carrying his lunch in a bag. He kept to himself. No one would ever have guessed this solitary man who walked from his home to his office was one of the richest men in the world.

By 1960, Ludwig's vast cash flow allowed him to invest in several other industries: oil refineries, coal, salt conversion, and real-estate development. It was one particular real-estate development that, for a short time, brought him into the limelight. It exposed his vast wealth and ultimately stained his reputation.

Ludwig always tried to predict the next big move. He was sure that natural resources like lumber, wood pulp, fruits, and vegetables would be in short supply. To capitalize on what he predicted to be a worldwide commodity shortage, Ludwig paid $3 million to a group of Brazilian families to purchase six thousand square miles of the remote Amazon rain forest. He cleared the dense forest and planted fast-growing trees, fruit orchards, and crops. He developed towns and roads. But the project was in trouble almost from the beginning. After he created thousands of miles of roads, several airstrips, a railway for freight, hospitals, towns, a deep-water port, and a gigantic parts and supply depot, he was forced to change his plans. The importing of the fast-growing gmelina super tree from Burma proved to be impractical. It was discovered that the gmelina couldn't grow in the soft soil of the Amazon. The shortage that he anticipated in lumber and wood pulp did not materialize either. Things went from bad to worse. Working from his New York office, Ludwig tried to give detailed instructions to his Amazon managers. But it became increasingly difficult to manage from afar, and Ludwig changed his mind and direction of the project constantly.

Between the inhospitable climate, his changing directions (thirty times in fourteen years), and the worldwide recession of the 1970s, the project was doomed. What started out as the largest and costliest entrepreneurial effort by a private individual became one of the largest failures in history. Ludwig lost over a billion dollars when he abandoned the Amazon. He was also vilified by the Brazilian public and environmentalists around the world because of his destruction of the rain forest.

Thanks to his other businesses, Ludwig still left the Amazon a very wealthy man. He developed the Princess hotel chain, the city of Westlake Village in California, salt mines in Mexico, and of course, the shipping industry. Additionally, he had investments in cattle ranching, insurance, and banking. Despite the loss of a billion dollars in the Amazon, all of his other investments led *Forbes* magazine to name Daniel Ludwig the world's richest person in 1982, after the deaths of fellow billionaires J. Paul Getty and Howard Hughes.

Ludwig refused to give interviews. He did not wear expensive clothes, shoes, or glasses. He preferred to travel alone, carry his own bags, and fly coach. When the emperor of Japan wanted to bestow Japan's highest honor, the Order of the Chrysanthemum, on Ludwig for his building of a Japanese shipyard that revived the shipping industry in Japan, Ludwig refused. Instead, he recommended that the honor be given to his shipyard manager.

Daniel Ludwig passed away in 1992. He left the large bulk of his foreign assets to the Ludwig Institute for Cancer Research in Switzerland. His US assets were left to the Virginia and D. K. Ludwig Fund for Cancer Research in New York. Since their founding, these organizations have provided grants in excess of $1 billion to further cancer research.

7 A Fight to the Death
Edwin Armstrong

There may never have been a corporate bully like the famous Radio Corporation of America. If you believe corporations control the power structure of the United States, you don't have to look too far back in history to see the abuse by one of America's largest and most influential companies. Now just a name and a trademark, it was once the face and driving force of one of the greatest and most important industries of modern times, broadcasting. The company is probably better known by its initials—RCA.

To truly understand RCA, you have to go back to the American Marconi Company in 1914, when bright engineers were performing groundbreaking experiments with radio waves just before World War I. The Marconi Company was in the wireless telegraph business. They had a near monopoly to use the airwaves for broadcasting messages in the United States.

At that time, a young man named Edwin Armstrong was working on a new invention. It was a new kind of electronic tube that he called a regenerative circuit. The new device would allow the transmission of not only telegraph strokes but also the RF signal from an antenna, which it would turn into audio waves, thus creating AM on the radio dial.

Armstrong patented what looked to be one of the greatest advancements in modern communication. However, the invention and patent turned out to be Armstrong's worst nightmare.

While Armstrong was filing his patent, another prolific inventor and engineer named Lee de Forest was also looking at ways to improve communication through wireless airwaves. While tinkering in his lab, using work that was pioneered by Armstrong, de Forest also stumbled on a method for converting RF signals into audio waves to amplify sound.

De Forest recognized the significance of this breakthrough, and in 1916, he rushed to file a patent for his own regenerative circuit. The subsequent fight over the two patents set up an epic battle that pitted some of the largest corporations in America against each other.

This wasn't the first time de Forest had found himself in a court battle over patent infringement. But this patent fight would go all the way to the Supreme Court. Meanwhile, another very real—and more important and deadly—battle had already begun in Europe. It was World War I that laid the groundwork for the Armstrong and de Forest drama to unfold.

At the start of World War I, the US government, under the orders of President Wilson, took control of the airwaves for national defense. Private companies were not allowed to broadcast on any wireless frequency for commercial purposes. All airwaves were to be used exclusively for and by the US government. The government even went so far as to suspend all radio patents. This caused an interruption of service by the American Marconi Company.

In 1919, after operations had halted in America while the war was raging in Europe, the British controlled the Marconi Company. They sought to purchase an Alexanderson alternator from General Electric to improve their business in Europe. Hearing of Marconi's request, Admiral W. H. G. Bullard of the US Navy went to meet with Owen D. Young, the president of GE. He requested that they not sell alternator equipment to

Marconi. As with any good conspiracy, evidence points to Young having contacted the federal government to help him facilitate the takeover of the radio business in the United States as a quid pro quo for killing the equipment sale to Marconi. That move pushed the foreign-owned Marconi out.

Admiral Bullard suggested that instead, General Electric should establish its own radio company in the United States. To facilitate this, the admiral secured a commercial monopoly on long-distance airwaves in the United States and delivered this monopoly to the new entity. Furthermore, he saw to it that the Marconi Company did not receive its operational licenses back and therefore was not allowed to resume operations in the United States after the war.

General Electric appreciated the tremendous opportunity placed before it. In 1919, the Radio Corporation of America (RCA) was formed. This shattered the Marconi Company, a part of which was the Marconi Wireless Telegraph Company of America that controlled the Pan-American Telegraph Company that, in turn, was controlled by the US Navy. It was there that a talented telegraph operator named David Sarnoff worked. Sarnoff became the general manager of RCA. In 1930, he was named RCA's president, which began his legendary career as one of the most powerful men in corporate America.

The US government not only controlled the airwaves during the war, but they also suspended the patents on all radio technology held by corporations to assure that new and important technology didn't get into the hands of the enemy. By this time, Armstrong and de Forest were in dire need of cash. They had filed endless patent lawsuits against each other. They both decided separately and independently to sell their patents to the large corporations that had the most to gain from the outcome of the trials.

De Forest sold his patent to AT&T. Armstrong sold his to Westinghouse. These two actions set the stage for the longest running patent dispute in history.

When the war ended, General Electric was ready and willing to take control of the airwaves—and also Marconi's remaining American assets. They were just not able to do so. GE's plans were stymied because they didn't control all of the necessary Armstrong and de Forest patents. GE's plans were further complicated by Armstrong's decision to partner with Westinghouse. There were now four large, hungry corporate powerhouses fighting to control all of the patents.

With the help and strong-arm tactics of Admiral Bullard, all of these powerful parties were coerced into pooling their respective patents into the Radio Corporation of America. This made RCA a government-created radio broadcasting and manufacturing monopoly for the sole benefit of General Electric, Westinghouse, and AT&T. It was no surprise that the admiral, for all of his work in wresting away Marconi's business and delivering it to three of the most powerful companies in the country, was awarded a seat on the board of directors of the newly formed RCA.

This didn't mean the parties would settle their patent disputes amicably. The case between Armstrong and de Forest and the companies that owned their patent rights went on for twelve years. It finally ended in the Supreme Court, where the court, which didn't really understand the technology, sided with de Forest. This decision was believed to be incorrect by the technical community—an opinion that was proven right when Irving Langmuir, an engineer and inventor with GE, explained how the technology worked. He proved that de Forest, who had created a successful tube that worked, did not have the slightest idea how the invention really worked. He had just gotten lucky using Armstrong's body of work.

Armstrong, as well as de Forest, went on to create a number of new patents for radio transmission. De Forest turned his attention away from RCA and did groundbreaking work for the movie industry. He went on to file many patents for the technology to make silent movies talk.

Armstrong, on the other hand, went on to develop the FM frequency for broadcasting that competed with AM. FM broadcasting offered far superior sound quality when compared to the AM frequency that was being broadcast by RCA.

This breakthrough again pitted Armstrong against insurmountable odds. This time, Armstrong's patents were solid. He felt confident traveling to the eighty-fifth floor of the Empire State Building to demonstrate the superior benefits to David Sarnoff, the president of RCA. Sarnoff was impressed, but he had his eye on a new medium—television—and declined to purchase Armstrong's patents.

Sarnoff was ruthless in his dealings in the early broadcast days. While Armstrong's was demonstrating his FM frequency on the eighty-fifth floor of the RCA building, Sarnoff was in another patent battle with a young inventor named Philo Farnsworth. Farnsworth was a high-school genius and electrical engineer who developed the plans for sending pictures and sound wirelessly to a receiver. Farnsworth had patented his invention for the television only to have it stolen from him by Sarnoff. See Farnsworth chapter 17

Turned down by RCA, Armstrong took his superior FM technology and financed his own FM stations. The first station was located in Alpine, New Jersey. This station's broadcast signal could be heard clearly for over one hundred miles. It used less power than the more conventional AM. Engineers of the day described it as "one of the most important radio developments since the first earphone crystal sets that were introduced."

This broadcast proved to be far enough and clear enough to reach the inner sanctum of RCA. With Farnsworth destroyed, the powerful RCA set its sights on Armstrong. Not wanting to buy Armstrong's patents, which would result in the payment of royalties, and with a desire to keep its monopoly on the airwaves, RCA lobbied the Federal Communications Commission (FCC) to change the regulations in a manner that would prevent FM from becoming a threat to AM.

Sarnoff also managed to get the FCC to move the FM radio spectrum from 40-50 MHz to 88-108 MHz. He reserved the 40 MHz spectrum, which Armstrong's stations and equipment used, for the eventual use of broadcasting television signals. This single FCC action rendered all of Armstrong's fifty FM stations—and half a million FM receivers—useless overnight.

The FCC's frequency change was supported not only by RCA but also by AT&T and Westinghouse. AT&T strongly supported the change, because the loss of Armstrong's FM relay stations forced the radio stations to buy wired links from AT&T.

RCA wasn't done with its attack on Armstrong. Sarnoff and RCA, as usual, exploited the inventions of brilliant minds like Armstrong and Farnsworth. The company filed a patent, in the name of RCA, for an FM system of its own. Armstrong then immediately sued RCA in yet another patent dispute that eventually left him penniless and emotionally drained.

RADIO CORPORATION OF AMERICA
RCA BUILDING
30 ROCKEFELLER PLAZA
NEW YORK 20, N. Y.

August 20, 1965

DAVID SARNOFF
CHAIRMAN OF THE BOARD

Mr. Steve Moore
Maywood
Olive Branch, Mississippi 38654

Dear Mr. Moore:

Thank you for your letter of
August 9 and for your kind observations about
the prologue I wrote -- "The Delusion of
Appeasement" -- for the book entitled --
"American Strategy for the Nuclear Age."

I appreciated hearing from
you and send you my best wishes.

Sincerely,

David Sarnoff

Document signed by David Sarnoff on RCA stationary

8 Boy, Can That Face Sell
Forrest Mars Sr.

M&M/Mars is one of the most recognizable names and largest family-owned companies in the world. Its candies—M&Ms, Snickers, and the Milky Way bar—are constantly the top-selling confections in the world. The worldwide growth of M&M/Mars can be traced not to its founder Frank Mars but to his son, Forrest Mars.

The start of this rich family history goes back to Franklin Clarence Mars and his wife, Ethel, who went into the wholesale candy business in Tacoma, Washington. The two didn't have great success until they moved the business to Minneapolis, Minnesota, and started to manufacture their own line of chocolate candies. It was then that Frank and Ethel created one of the best-selling candy bars in the world, the Milky Way.

Milky Way was the first "filled" chocolate bar of its time. This unique feature made it a huge success almost from the start. The first year, it yielded $7,000 in sales; just a few years later, sales topped $700,000. The small factory was soon yielding more money than the couple had ever dreamed possible.

To garner even more sales, Frank moved his family to Chicago. In the early part of the twentieth century, Chicago was the center of the candy-making industry because of its central location and access to rail traffic. It was in Chicago that Frank brought his son, Forrest Mars, into the business after the young man graduated from Yale.

From the beginning, father and son had a very strained relationship. Forrest was constantly trying to encourage his father to expand globally. Frank wasn't interested. He was content with domestic growth. He didn't want to "risk" the company with "unnecessary" foreign expansion. Forrest, on the other hand, was getting increasingly restless. He was upset with the way his father ran the business.

By 1933, Frank and Forrest were at odds. If Forrest wanted to expand globally, he would have to do it on his own. So Frank gave Forrest the foreign rights, the recipe for the Milky Way bar, and $50,000. The caveat was that Forrest couldn't use the name Milky Way. Armed with the money and the Milky Way recipe, Forrest headed to England to manufacture his new candy line. He named it the Mars Bar.

Forrest's first order of business was to learn all he could about candy making, especially the process of making chocolate. Before jumping into manufacturing, he took jobs as an apprentice for some of the best chocolate makers in the world: Nestlé and Tobler. As surprising as it may seem now, his father's company, Mars Inc., did not make its own chocolate. The company bought the chocolate wholesale, like many other candy makers of that time. The chocolate company of choice for all was none other than the Hersey Chocolate Company. (See Hershey chapter 16)

Forrest did what his father wouldn't do: he expanded globally. He was a ferocious deal maker. Before long his company, Mars Ltd., was making not only candy but also pet food and rice.

Forrest was a marketing genius. During the 1930s, '40s and '50s, Forrest concentrated on marketing, advertising, and brand-building. It was Forrest's marketing methods in business that eventually led Mars to overtake Hershey as the leader in worldwide candy sales.

In England, Mars became interested in a new method for converting and cooking rice. The process, which sealed the flavor and nutrients into the rice kernels after the husk was removed, was a breakthrough in food processing. Forrest saw great possibilities in the method, and he bought the company that had developed the revolutionary process. Indeed, the process was new but, to Forrest's way of thinking, it was still a commodity that had no brand identity to set it apart. Forrest was about to change all that.

Forrest's father, Frank, died in 1933, only a year after Forrest left for Europe. Forrest didn't return to the United States until 1940, seven years after his father's death. He was well-established in Europe and felt comfortable enough to come back. Although he now owned a controlling interest in the Mars Company after his father's death, the Mars company in USA was still his competitor. Since he didn't have the rights to sell the Milky Way in the United States (what he called the Mars Bar), he brought two other products back with him that would eventually change the world.

The first of these products was the process for converted rice. Forrest needed a way to make his rice stand out from other bulk commodities. He wanted to position it as a convenient, recognizable branded food for every kitchen.

During a routine lunch with one of his lawyers in Chicago, he brought up his rice idea. He explained that he was trying to package it as a food women would easily recognize and buy every time they went into a store. His attorney offhandedly remarked that the only way anyone would buy the product was if a man was selling it. As an example, he pointed to Frank Brown, the black maitre d' in the restaurant. Forrest instantly recognized the potential. From that day on, having borrowed the name from a renowned rice farmer, Frank Brown became known as Uncle Ben, and Uncle Ben became forever synonymous with rice. That lunch inspired the first branded commodity product in the world. Since that time, brand names have been added to thousands of products that were once only sold in bulk.

The second innovation Forrest brought with him was an idea for candy that he had come across during the 1930s Spanish Civil War. Soldiers were eating a chocolate pellet that had been coated with a hard candy shell so the chocolate wouldn't melt. Up to that time, stores without air-conditioning had trouble stocking chocolate candy during the summer months. If Forrest could create a chocolate that wouldn't melt in the heat, he could capture a very large share of the market. Thus, the candy with the unforgettable slogan "melts in your mouth, not in your hands" received its first patent in 1941.

That year, 1941, marked the beginning of the war years. Rationing was already implemented in the United States in order to save resources for the military. Chocolate was no exception. If Forrest was going to introduce his new candy in 1941, he would need a dependable supply of chocolate. He turned to his friends at Hershey.

Hershey was supplying chocolate to the military, so it had access to whatever was needed to produce chocolate for the troops. Even Frank's Mars Inc. was dependant on Hershey for its bulk chocolate. To secure a steady supply of chocolate, Forrest approached the son of the president of Hershey, Bruce Murrie. Frank asked for Murrie's help to get a reliable supply of bulk chocolate. To compensate Murrie, Forrest offered him a 20 percent share of the new candy. Murrie agreed. Thus, Hershey supplied the chocolate, sugar, and technology for the new brand. When the war was over and the candy was already manufactured and on the market, Forrest was quick to buy back Murrie's share.

According to the "official" history as presented by M&M/Mars, the name M&M is a combination of these two individuals—the first "M" for Forrest Mars, the second for Bruce Murrie. That's the official story.

There is a second, unauthorized history that has floated around from time to time. It is that M&M doesn't stand for Mars and

Murrie at all, but rather for Mars and Mars. After all, it was in 1940 that Forrest Mars made his triumphant return to the United States and re-established ties with his family. M&M could very easily stand for the commemorating of two great people in the candy business, Frank and Forrest Mars.

9 You're In, You're Out, You're In, You're Out, You're Out!: Harry Snyder

Every now and then, the word *cult* attaches itself to a movement. On occasion, the word might also be associated with wines, stores, or restaurants. One California business that has what might be described as a "cult following" is a small fast-food restaurant chain called In–N-Out Burger.

In-N-Out is the creation of Harry Snyder and his wife, Esther. Together they created a fast-food chain that even makes Ronald McDonald's mouth water.

Movies stars, congressmen, senators, sports figures, and plain old folks have all made a pilgrimage to one of In-N-Out's three-hundred-plus West Coast locations. Some even order off the restaurant's "secret menu" to prove they are one of the regulars. The chain has been mentioned in Academy Award speeches, on the *Tonight Show*, and in numerous other television shows and movies.

In-N-Out doesn't pay for that kind of high-profile publicity. They earn it by keeping things simple and making great burgers, fries, and shakes.

So how did a small burger chain get so famous that Jennifer Garner from the TV show *Alias* mentioned it on the Academy Awards show? It all goes back to Harry and Esther.

When Harry started In-N-Out in 1948, he actually had a partner. Hamburger stands and drive-ins were popping up all over the country after the war. Harry was ready to capitalize on this. But, as often happens, he and his partner had very different visions. Harry's partner wanted fast growth, and Harry wanted to take a slower approach. Thus, Harry became fed up with his partner and bought him out.

Harry's initial store was one of the first fast-food burger stands to offer the now-popular drive-thru concept. This is not to be confused with the drive-ins of the early days.

Harry envisioned customers driving *in* to a lane and *out* the other side with their burgers. He didn't expect people to eat on the premises. That was the genesis of the main In-N-Out Burger concept. Harry was very mechanical and used his skills to hook up a two-way speaker system. This allowed customers to stay in their cars and place their orders directly with the kitchen. The customer would then drive through and pick up the order at another window. In the year 1948, this was considered a novel approach. It was the first use of a two-way radio to place and take orders at a fast-food operation. To move traffic through faster, Harry had cars pass in double lines on each side of the kitchen.

Harry's go-slow approach was contrary to what others in the fast food burger business were doing during the grow grow grow of the 1950's. While restaurants were opening dozens of stores, Harry was content to open a new store only after he had earned enough money to pay for the store in cash. While his competitors added items to their menus, Harry held fast to his simple menu, saying that he "was going to do just one thing and do it the best it can be done … burgers, fries and shakes." Harry agonized for over two years as whether or not he should add Dr Pepper to the menu.

Harry focused on burgers and fries. He was adamant that the burgers had to be made from fresh ground beef—never frozen—and grilled to order. Fries had to be hand-cut at the restaurant from a potato that either he or Esther had inspected for size and quality. Shakes were only made with real, fresh ice cream. When others were paying minimum wage to their employees, Harry paid his 20 to 30 percent higher than the competition in order to attract the best people.

Because the grill was the most important part of the operation, Harry trusted only himself to grill the burgers. It took months, maybe years, before Harry was comfortable enough to promote an employee to the highest position of Grill Operator. All employees had to be bright and dedicated. While other fast-food giants saw employees turn over every six months, Harry's staff stayed for years. Many made In-N-Out their full-time career.

Harry was a tough boss who was liked by everyone. He was always there to help. He often provided food for free to help out with a fundraiser for a good cause or just to help someone who was down and out. He was the same way with his family.

Harry and Esther had two sons. Both were expected to learn the business. Rich, the youngest son, wanted to be involved. Guy, on the other hand, was much more interested in hot rods, an interest he developed when Harry was talked into buying 50 percent of a local drag strip. Of course, Harry sold In-N-Out Burgers there. It was from then on that In-N-Out was not only associated with sedans rolling into drive-thrus but also hot rods and fast cars in general.

By the 1950s, Harry had managed to build and pay for six stores. This was about the same time that a milkshake-machine salesman by the name of Ray Kroc was starting to franchise the McDonald Brothers hamburger chain. Ray was planning to open thousands of stores around the world. Harry was still training his next manager at the grill with hopes of moving him to store number seven. Harry was approached by Ray Kroc and many other fast-talking investors who all wanted him to expand the McDonald's way. Harry wasn't interested. Doing one thing well and growing slowly with no debt, while keeping the entire operation in the family, was what Harry wanted.

To keep quality up and products fresh, Harry opened an In-N-Out commissary warehouse across the street from his first store. The plan was to bring in the beef, produce, and other supplies each day, personally inspect them, and then and only then send these fresh fully inspected supplies out to all the stores. Each store would get the proper fresh supplies delivered each morning. In order to do this, all of the stores had to be within driving distance of the warehouse. This system is still in place today, which is one of the reasons that growth is still slow. Every potato, head of lettuce, and tomato is inspected for size and quality. If it doesn't measure up, it is sent back. Tomatoes must be a certain size, and only the center of the tomato is used to ensure that each customer gets the perfect burger each and every time.

By the 1970s, Harry had opened eighteen In-N-Out Burgers and was happy with the growth. The In-N-Out locations were highly successful and very profitable. It was at that time that Harry found out he had lung cancer and didn't have long to live. Harry started making plans to see to it that In-N-Out would survive him and stay in the family. He set up several trusts. He gave control of the restaurants to his wife, Esther, and his youngest son, Rich. Guy, his oldest son, received a small minority share. It was clear to Harry that Guy, after suffering a bad drag-racing accident, would not be able to operate the business the way Harry wanted. Guy had been hooked on drugs and alcohol and ran with a wild crowd. Rich, on the other hand, was more like Harry, conservative and thoughtful.

In 1976, Harry passed away. Rich, at twenty-four years old, became the president of the eighteen stores in the In-N-Out Burger chain. This pushed Guy further from the family and deeper into destructive behavior.

Rich settled into the job with zeal and planned a new expansion program. He embraced religion and even brought his religious values into the company. It was his idea to put numbers that related to Bible passages on the hamburger wrappers and cups. Another idea was a secret handshake known only to the regulars. Rich needed to balance growth with his father's motto and values: "Do one thing well, make it fresh for the customer, and pay employees well."

Rich's plan was to build eight to twelve new locations a year using the cash flow from the company. By the 1990s, under Rich's leadership, In-N-Out had expanded—but Rich did keep his promise to his father. Each In-N-Out served the same quality simple menu the same way his father's first store did in 1948.

In 1993, Rich, Esther, and three other In-N-Out executives who had been with the company since the beginning went to Fresno, California, to celebrate the opening of store number ninety-three. Every new In-N-Out Burger store is celebrated the same way. There is no fancy advertising or promotion, but the owners and company executives are always present. It is their cars that are the first to roll through the drive-thru. Following them in most cases is a line so long it snarls traffic for hours.

When the Fresno opening was complete, everyone headed back to the office. Rich and Esther were to take a chartered flight, and the other four executives were scheduled on a commercial flight. Just before Rich and his mother were to take off on the plane, the others decided to join them because of flight delays at the Fresno airport. The first stop was to drop Esther off close to home before the rest continued to the new offices in Orange County. After a brief goodbye to Esther, the group was again airborne. On the second leg of the flight, the pilot was warned by the Orange County tower that he was flying too fast and was in danger of catching up to a 757 jet that was on approach to the Orange County Airport. Mile by mile, they got closer to the jet. The pilots were aware that they were closing in on the jet, but they felt they were still at a safe distance. Less than a mile from the runway, at low altitude, the charter jet got caught in the wake of the 757 and flipped over. The plane crashed. Everyone on board was killed instantly.

The loss was devastating. All of the upper management and the owner of In-N-Out were dead. Esther, at seventy-three years old, rushed back to headquarters to take control. The trust documents stated that only a blood family member could inherit Rich's share of the company. Rich had been married just over a year before he died, and he had no children. The next of kin was Guy, Rich's older brother. To the fear and anguish of all of the employees at In-N-Out, Esther announced that Guy was to be the new president and owner.

At first, Guy made an effort to run the company. He continued the expansion that Rich had started. He seemed to have kicked the drugs and alcohol, but it didn't last. Guy stopped showing up for work and soon increased his drug usage. Esther was left to run the company. When the police found Guy passed out drunk in his car on the highway, everyone breathed a sigh of relief that the news wasn't printed in the Orange County newspapers. Guy alternated sleeping at friends' houses, in a camper, or at his ex-wife and daughter's house until they threw him out. Guy was on a downward spiral at the same time In-N-Out was struggling to recover from the loss of its charismatic leader.

In 1999, just six years after his brother died in the devastating plane crash, Guy passed away of a heart attack bought on by years of drug and alcohol abuse. The officers who arrived on the scene and saw the disheveled and unkempt body concluded in their report that the man they found dead that day was a pauper who was unemployed and destitute. In actuality, the lifeless body they came upon was that of a millionaire, Guy Snyder, the sole owner of one of the most famous and successful fast-food burger chains in the West. In-N-Out, by the time of Guy's death, was making tens of millions of dollars in profits each year.

Esther was now seventy-nine and alone. Without her boys and her husband, she still owned the family business. Although Guy had divorced years earlier and Didn't have much contact with his estranged daughter due to his addiction, she was the only blood family heir. All of Guy's shares in the company went to her. At the age of seventeen, Lynsi Snyder was the only living heir of one of America's largest fast-food fortunes. Under the terms of the trust, she received all of the stock in the company in intervals that started on her twenty-first birthday. She would get full control of the company after Esther passed away.

It was after Lynsi's twenty-third birthday that a long time In-N-Out employee, Rich Boyd, a close family friend and co-trustee of the Snyder estate, filed a lawsuit against Lynsi. The suit alleged that Lynsi was trying to push both he and Esther out of the company in order to gain full control. Once again In-N-Out's dirty laundry was aired in court.

Esther died in 2006 at the age of eighty-six, in the midst of the lawsuit. The case was promptly settled, and Esther's granddaughter, Lynsi Snyder Martinez, was in sole control of a true American icon.

10 So Much for Cars
Henry Ford

Henry Ford is probably one of the most recognizable names in American history. The Ford name has been synonymous with automobiles for almost a hundred years. You can ask people from Michigan to Macau—most of them have heard of Henry Ford, associate the Ford name with cars, and identify Henry Ford as the founder of the Ford Motor Company. You wouldn't associate the name Ford with agricultural products such as soybeans, but you would be wrong not to.

The truth is that the Model T that Henry Ford developed and manufactured, plus the sophisticated automobiles that the Ford Motor Company manufactures today, are only a small part of the Henry Ford story.

Henry Ford was born on a farm in a rural part of Detroit, Michigan, in 1863. Henry hated the farm. It wasn't the farmland that Henry disliked but the work that went into running a farm. In the 1800s, working on a farm was backbreaking work from sunup to sundown. There were no tractors to ride in order to till the fields. There were only horses that the workers had to walk behind. Henry hated horses. It was those horses Henry hated that inspired him to create his famed Model T automobile.

From an early age, Henry showed an aptitude for mechanics. The first use of his mechanical skills came when his father gave him a pocket watch for his fifteenth birthday. Curiosity about how things worked prompted Henry to open the back of the watch and disassemble it. He then reassembled it in perfect working order. Henry became so proficient at disassembling and assembling timepieces that his reputation spread to friends and neighbors who said that young Henry could fix a watch with his eyes closed.

After his mother's death, Henry realized the only thing that had been keeping him on the farm was the love he had for his mother. With his mother gone, Henry saw no reason to stay on the farm to continue the backbreaking work he saw as dehumanizing. He decided to travel to Detroit and apprentice as a machinist.

When his three-year apprenticeship ended, he returned to the farm and his rural roots. Despite his hatred for farmwork, the rural lifestyle held a fascination for Henry that continued throughout his life.

After several years, Henry took a job with Westinghouse. He worked on the new portable steam engines that were popping up on rural farms as labor-saving devices.

With the introduction of the first automobiles on the streets of Detroit, Henry became interested in gasoline power. He immediately recognized that the gasoline-powered automobile, with some modifications, could be used to replace the dreadful horses and would ease the lives of the farmers. Henry began experimenting with gasoline engines with the hope of making his own horseless carriage. His experiments paid off when on June 4, 1896, he test-drove the Ford Quadricycle. It was a carriage on four bicycle tires that was propelled by a gasoline engine.

The race was on to build cars in Detroit. Everyone wanted to be part of the excitement. Henry was no exception. He wanted to get into the car business full time. He met with some prominent Detroit business leaders who were willing to stake him in the automobile manufacturing business. Henry and his investors incorporated the Detroit Automobile Company on August 5, 1899.

From the beginning, Henry and his investors were at odds. They each had different goals. The investors wanted to produce as many cars as possible to compete with the very successful Oldsmobile that had a curved dash. Henry saw the business as a laboratory in which to perfect his designs.

By 1901, Henry Ford had produced only twenty automobiles at a cost of $86,000 ($2.1 million in today's dollars). This caused the stockholders to refuse further funding for Henry's experiments and, consequently, the company.

Ford was undaunted. He would not put an automobile into production until it was free of flaws. Henry did create several race cars using many of his innovations. His success on the racetrack caught the eye of another group of investors. With his newfound investors and the remaining assets of the Detroit Automobile Company, Henry got back to business, re-naming his company the Henry Ford Company.

By 1902, Henry still hadn't produced a successful car. However, all was not lost for the investors in the Henry Ford Company. They ousted Henry Ford and brought in Henry Leland to run the company and produce cars with Henry Ford's designs. In 1902, the company changed its name, for the final time, to the Cadillac Automobile Company. Today, everyone knows it as the luxury automobile division of General Motors.

A year later, Henry Ford was up and running again. This time, the company was known as the Ford Motor Company. The new investors were more patient than the previous groups. They let Henry tinker to perfect his automobile. The Ford Motor Company only produced a few hand-built cars a day in the early years. That was just fine with Henry. He enjoyed spending time in his laboratory experimenting, with a grander idea in mind.

Finally, in 1908, Henry Ford perfected the vision that had come to him while on the farm. Henry imagined a car that could go on virtually any road, was simple to build and reliable, and just about everyone could afford. Thus, the Model T was born.

Within a few years, the Ford Motor Company was making $60 million a year in profits. Henry didn't want to give any of the money to his stockholders. Henry Ford was on his way to becoming the richest man in America.

With his newfound wealth, Henry was now able to experiment in social areas. His socialistic views and his drive to make money culminated in his reputation as the pioneer of "capitalist Welfare." Henry Ford's fame came when he shocked the business world with the five-dollar-a-day job. He went even further when he set up a department within the Ford factory that followed employees home to check on their welfare and make sure they were living a proper life. He became obsessed with making sure that his employees lived in the "Ford manner."

Henry was always looking for ways to build a better car. At the same time, he wanted to lower the cost to his customers, thereby allowing more and more people to buy his cars. Interestingly enough, as more people bought and owned his Model T and left the farms for the big city, the more Henry missed the farm and the rural life. This led Ford to build Greenfield Village, where he recreated the rural town of his youth.

Although Henry hated farming, he did like the rural farm life. He always felt that agriculture and industry were natural partners that could, and should, work together to give people a better life. The industry was for the cash needed, and the farm was for the livelihood of the people. He was indeed a unique man of many contradictions.

Henry Ford was one of the first people in the world to think about sustainability. You might even call him an environmentalist of sorts, despite the fact that his cars would one day be the single most polluting invention on the planet.

During the Depression and into World War II, Ford set up and maintained a laboratory to create products from vegetables, mainly soybeans. He was successful in creating all types of products from soybeans. During the war years of the 1940s, he successfully built a car out of soy plastics that was powered by ethanol made from soy. Even the suit he wore was made out of soy fibers. Although Henry didn't see success from these ideas, his experiments were very beneficial to mankind. His laboratory was instrumental in creating many of the products made from soybeans that we enjoy today.

Henry Ford came full circle when, in 1922, he purchased the luxury automobile brand Lincoln Motors. He purchased the company out of bankruptcy from none other than Henry Leland. It was Henry Leland, you might remember, who was brought in by the investors of the original Henry Ford Company in 1902 that resulted in Henry Ford's firing.

11 Up in Smoke and Mirrors: Ivar Kreuger

In the early part of the twentieth century, there were several men who dominated their respective fields and became household names.

J. P. Morgan dominated banking and lending to foreign governments. Andrew Carnegie controlled the largest steelmaking company, which was one day to become U. S. Steel. John D. Rockefeller monopolized the oil and gas business. One name that is absent from most lists, but is possibly one of the most influential of the time, was that of a Swede, Ivar Kreuger, known as the Match King.

From 1922 to 1932, there wasn't a more famous person in the world than Kreuger. He appeared on numerous magazine covers, including *Time*. There were articles written about him in newspapers and magazines in six different countries describing his many exploits. Kreuger was not only involved in the manufacture of matches, but he was also the first to create a complete vertical integration for manufacturing matches in countries around the world.

Kreuger's company, Swedish Match, owned mines, timber, paper, and chemical companies that furnished all of the elements used in the manufacturing of matches. With the money his companies earned, he branched out into lending money to governments, filmmakers, and construction and mining companies. He also invested in real estate and agriculture.

Kreuger's beginnings were very modest. After earning an engineering degree in Sweden, he set sail to America to make his fortune. Unfortunately, success and good fortune were not to be found on that trip. After working for several building contractors he felt were inferior to him, Kreuger decided to return to his native Sweden to search for work. It was there that he was introduced to Paul Toll, a small reputable contractor who had big dreams. Kreuger, with his enthusiasm, charm, and innovative ways, proved to be a good match for Toll, and they became partners.

The partnership they formed was called Kreuger and Toll. Kreuger was a master at getting business. He came up with unique propositions for his clients. Contractors were billing clients for material and labor and, of course, profit. But if there were any job delays, the risk was always borne by the client. If contractors dragged their feet and delayed the job, the client just had to pay more. Only the reputation of the contractor assured that a job would be completed on time. Kreuger saw it another way. He believed that clients would pay more if they were assured the project would be finished on a specified date. To back up his guarantee, Kreuger promised to pay the clients a penalty if a job ran overtime. Conversely, he required a bonus from the client if the project was finished early. This was a first for the construction industry.

Soon, Kreuger and Toll were building some of Sweden's most important and beautiful buildings, both public and private. To fuel growth, they borrowed extensively from a syndicate of Sweden's largest banks. With the cash flowing in, Kreuger created a holding company and started to purchase numerous other businesses. One of those businesses was the small match-manufacturing plant where Kreuger's father worked. Kreuger saw great possibilities in match production—especially the manufacturing of safety matches, which were invented in Sweden.

Safety matches are matches that will only light if they are struck on a special strip located on the side of the accompanying box. These matches were cheap to make and became a "must have" for almost every person in the world. Matches were used to light fires for cooking, candles, tobacco, and many other essentials of the time.

Although matches were needed by everyone and were cheap to make, they were also easy to manufacture. This meant that there was little barrier to entry, which prompted many enterprising men around the world to get into the match-making business. Sweden alone had over a dozen companies that manufactured matches. Brutal competition drove prices down and caused profit margins to drop to almost nothing. Kreuger's plan was to buy up all the factories that made matches so he would create a monopoly to drive up prices. A penny or two profit per box of matches would be enough to make the business very successful. With the product being so cheap, consumers could still afford to buy matches even if the price was increased by two cents a box. Kreuger named his first acquisition Swedish Match.

Kreuger's plan worked flawlessly. After slightly more than two years, Kreuger claimed to control over 80 percent of the Swedish match business. By manufacturing billions of matches a year, he was able to export to dozens of countries around the globe at a very low price. Kreuger was sure he could duplicate this monopoly in other countries. But to succeed in America, the largest market in the world, was another story.

America had outlawed monopolies. Getting a foothold there would be difficult. The largest player in the United States was the Diamond Match Company. Diamond didn't have a monopoly in the United States. It did have a very large market share, and it was profitable. Kreuger wanted to own Diamond Match. To make this happen, he established a US company and then hired someone to represent him in his dealings with Diamond Match.

Diamond was interested until its auditors/accountants, Price Waterhouse, warned about the dubious financial statements

Kreuger had submitted. The reports just didn't add up. Price Waterhouse couldn't make them balance. Kreuger's representative resubmitted the documents with revised numbers, which only added to the confusion. Thus, the deal was off. For the second time, Kreuger left America having failed in his objective.

All this worldwide growth didn't come without a cost. The bank syndicates who financed Kreuger's expansion were starting to get concerned. Much too much money was being lent to Kreuger and Toll and to Swedish Match. Many of the bankers were concerned that the syndicates' exposure was way too high. They demanded that the lead bank hire an accounting firm to perform an audit of Kreuger's companies, a task that would be very difficult to perform.

Kreuger had used some new and innovative financial tools to expand and finance Swedish Match. By all accounts, Kreuger was the first to create "special purpose" companies designed to remove certain liabilities from a firm's balance sheet, thus hiding those liabilities from lenders and stockholders. These special-purpose vehicles were the same as those used by Enron eighty years later to increase profits and hide debt exposure from stockholders and auditors. Unable to make sense of Kreuger's books, the banks ultimately decided that Kreuger would have to find money elsewhere.

Kreuger was sure he could come up with what he needed for Swedish Match. He was going to try America again. This time he orchestrated his entrance. He hired actors from his movie company and departed on a ship to New York. While on board the ship, he and his cast of actors made sure the passengers were well aware of the successful Ivar Kreuger. By the time the ship made port on the shores of the United States, everyone on board wanted to invest with the Swedish Match King.

Kreuger's plan was not yet complete. He still needed an American banker to finance his endeavors. For that he paid a Swedish banker to introduce him to Lee, Higginson and Company of Boston.

Lee, Higginson (as it was known) was at that time one of the oldest and largest banking houses in the United States—smaller than J. P. Morgan, but bigger then Goldman, Lehman, Loeb, and all the other firms on Wall Street. Kreuger's choice of Lee, Higginson was not a coincidence. Higginson was far enough from Wall Street—where, just a few years earlier, he had embarrassed himself with Price Waterhouse and Diamond Match—that there was less of a chance that the firm would have heard of the questionable financial statements and charges leveled against him by the accountants at Price Waterhouse.

As it turned out, Higginson was the perfect choice. The blue-blood, white-shoe firm was fascinated by Kreuger and marveled at his business exploits. He described a very unusual and innovative proposition that would be very profitable for their firm. Kreuger explained that he was the largest worldwide manufacturer of safety matches, and he wanted to monopolize the industry. He explained that although he couldn't monopolize the US market, he could control other international markets where monopolies were legal.

To entice investors into buying the stock in his American company, Kreuger claimed they could invest in his American match company and share in the profits from his other match businesses around the globe. He had a very clever plan to accomplish this feat. Kreuger was going to start a new company in America called the International Match Company. He wanted Lee, Higginson to sell a new type of debenture. This would be similar to a bond paying 6.5 percent, and there would also be profit sharing with International Match. This was the derivative of its day. Kreuger went on to explain that he was going to use the money raised by the offering to lend money to foreign governments. This would be done in exchange for a monopoly to sell matches in their respective countries.

Kreuger explained to the partners at Higginson that the security on the bonds would be the loans to the foreign governments. The interest paid would match the interest being paid on the loan.

The money earned by International Match would be the profit it received from a monopoly on matches. These profits, according to Kreuger, would be substantial because of the pricing power held by the monopolies. The Lee, Higginson partners loved the idea, and so did the public. The new American gold debentures issued by International Match were oversold before they were even issued. The price after issue soared. Investors quickly realized that the bonds paid a significantly higher return because they shared in the profits earned by selling matches, which was a product that everyone understood and used. Kreuger was indeed a visionary, as this scheme is exactly the one used by the major banks in the subprime real-estate debacle of 2008.

The success of the debentures allowed Kreuger to go head to head with the most famous international banker in the world, J. P. Morgan. At first, Morgan wasn't concerned. When it became clear that Kreuger was more than a little successful in selling securities and raising millions of dollars to finance his lending to foreign governments in exchange for match monopolies, Morgan did become concerned—and more than a little suspicious. Long-standing relationships that Morgan had with governments started to break as Krueger offered these governments more money at lower prices than the House of Morgan. Kreuger not only lowered the interest paid by the governments, he also offered profit sharing in International Match to the borrowing countries. This potentially covered their payments on Krueger's loans.

Kreuger was fast becoming one of the most famous men on two continents. His companies employed 26,000 people. He controlled the match trade in over twenty countries. He owned over two hundred companies, including Sweden's number-one telephone company, LM Ericsson. By 1929, Kreuger was one of the richest men in the world. He had an estimated net worth of 30 billion Swedish Kronor, the equivalent of $100 billion today. To put it in perspective, the total loans for all of Sweden's banks total only four billion Swedish Kronor.

Everyone wanted a piece of Herr Kreuger. With the help of a beautiful sixteen-year-old blond girl named Greta Garbo, whom he had discovered in a hat shop at Sweden's major department store, even his movie production company was soaring. Kreuger dated Garbo, and the two frequently dined with Mary Pickford and Douglas Fairbanks, two of the most famous actors of the day. Kreuger entertained royalty and titans of finance, and even had a Rockefeller on his board of directors.

The deals with Lee, Higginson were getting larger and larger. Lee, Higginson did show concern about the size of the operation. The firm also became concerned about Kreuger's secretiveness with regard to his dealings. Once again, the issue of his previous financial problems surfaced and became a point of friction. Higginson did have some comfort in the fact that Kreuger had hired the accounting firm of Ernst and Ernst to do his books. But the books were getting harder and harder to figure out. International Match entries became increasingly difficult to decipher. Ernst and Ernst, for its part, was relying on Swedish Match accountants in Sweden to keep things straight. This was a large task, given that Krueger had so many companies to control. Kreuger seemed to be the only one who understood the vast complexities of the operation and the numerous special-purpose companies he had established in order to lower the companies' taxes.

The Lee, Higginson partners felt a little more at ease when they read the report that Ernst and Ernst provided detailing its discussions with the Swedish accountants in regard to Swedish Match. This was coupled with the success the public was having with the securities issued by International Match and Kreuger's other companies that he had established in America. The securities were paying dividends of 12 to 30 percent, not including the rising prices of the shares.

On October 28, 1929, Kreuger's fame and success put him on the cover of *Time* magazine. However, October 28, 1929, was also the day of the largest crash in stock-market history. Some say it ushered in the Great Depression. Surprisingly, Kreuger's preferred shares dropped very little. By the time the article in *Time* hit the newsstands, International Match shares and his other securities were actually rising. This only added to the mystique of Ivar Kreuger.

Everyone could understand the match business. Kreuger's securities were backed by foreign government loans. Most of the major Wall Street bankers and some foreign banks held shares in International Match and Kreuger's American Swedish Match, so they weren't prone to panic like many individual investors. Kreuger even managed to sell a $50 million offering after the crash to eager investors. When the underwriters found that over 40 percent of subscribers weren't able to buy the securities from the underwriting banks, Kreuger agreed to buy them back in a year at a profit. With Swedish Match's strong cash flow, the bankers were satisfied and didn't panic.

Two years after the stock-market crash and with America in a depression, Kreuger was still making deals and paying extraordinarily high dividends to his investors. In 1930 and 1931, while stocks prices were falling, Kreuger's securities and the profits of his match companies were actually rising. In 1931, he decided to sell his ownership in LM Ericsson to ITT International Telephone & Telegraph. ITT paid Kreuger $11 million as a down payment, plus a promise of ITT stock as soon as the transaction closed. A routine audit by ITT's auditors, Price Waterhouse, discovered that L. M. Ericsson's cash account was misrepresented. In place of the cash were cheap, worthless foreign bonds that Kreuger had entered in at full par value. Kreuger admitted he had taken a loan from Ericsson and replaced the cash with bonds. He disputed the value and said it must be an issue of translation. In any event, the bonds were guaranteed by him, and he soon bought the bonds back.

The president of ITT didn't care about Kreuger's guarantee. Neither did its bankers, J. P. Morgan and City National Bank. City National notified Lee, Higginson about the irregularities in the Ericsson deal. When they met with Kreuger in his apartment on Park Avenue in New York, he assured them it was a matter of translation. Just six days after that meeting, a $4 million unsecured loan came due for International Match. With the Depression deepening around the world and without a way to issue more securities or borrow, Kreuger had to admit he couldn't pay the loan. Most of the banks involved, including National City, were aware of the failure of the Ericsson deal and agreed to renew the loan. The more conservative Mellon Bank would not. Mellon insisted on cash collateral. The banks reduced the $4 million note by $200,000. Kreuger provided 350,000 shares of Diamond Match, which he had finally managed to acquire, as collateral. Both the banks and Lee, Higginson were happy with the agreement.

With money growing short, Kreuger turned to Riksbank, also known as the Bank of Sweden, the oldest central bank in the world. He wanted to borrow more money in order to keep his operations going and meet the deadlines for dividend payments. Despite his financial statements showing millions upon millions in profits and assets, Kreuger was starting to have a hard time paying the interest on his many securities. Riksbank, after looking at Kreuger's financial statements, became concerned. They were inclined not to grant more loans. Kreuger already had outstanding loans with the bank in excess of half of all the reserve currency in Sweden. With such a large exposure, the chairman of the bank requested a meeting with Krueger in Berlin. Looking pale, Kreuger left America and arrived in Paris for a meeting with his leading Swedish banker, Oscar Rydbeck.

Following the meeting with Rydbeck, Kreuger wasn't feeling well and made a visit to his doctor. He was told he didn't look good and needed to care for himself. Kreuger left the doctor and retired to his Paris apartment. There, Kreuger lay back in his bed, took a gun from the drawer, and shot himself in the heart. He left a note for his creditors that read, "I have made such a mess of things …. Goodbye now and thanks I. K." Ivar Kreuger was dead at fifty-two.

The news of Kreuger's death caused a panic in Sweden and on Wall Street. When receivers appointed by the Swedish government took over the Kreuger empire, they were shocked to find most of the supposed monopolies were nonexistent. Kreuger only managed to secure two true monopolies for Swedish Match. Furthermore, International Match's assets consisted of worthless notes from two of Kreuger's sham companies. The bonds that the banks and investors held as security were also elaborate forgeries that were created by Kreuger. Swedish Match did exist and produced 60 percent of the world's matches, but it wasn't making anywhere near the money Kreuger had claimed. It couldn't even come up with the money needed to pay the dividends. It seemed that Kreuger was paying high dividends to his investors using money he generated from new investors and new bank loans. The Swedish receivers, aided by J. P. Morgan and Company, eventually found that Kreuger's vast empire was nothing more than a giant pyramid scheme similar to the one Charles Ponzi had created two years before Krueger entered the United States (Bernie Madoff meets Lehman Brothers).

Kreuger's original company, the one he started with Paul Toll, was not part of the holding company. It therefore managed to come through the Kreuger crash intact. Paul Toll grew the company through an acquisition of his own. He was one of the leading commercial builders in Sweden. Toll eventually renamed the company AB Toll Construction and continued operating into the 1990s.

Lee, Higginson didn't fare as well. Higginson, the second largest and one of the oldest investment houses in the world, was forced to close its doors a year after Kreuger took his life. It took receivers over nine years to untangle the Kreuger empire. In the end, though, Kreuger did leave some impressive accomplishments.

Swedish Match was rescued by an emergency loan from the Swedish government in 1933. The company still exists today as a successful international match and tobacco manufacturer headquartered in Sweden. Kreuger, of course, is also remembered as the greatest swindler of all times, having stolen more than $1 billion from his investors.

The magnitude of Kreuger's securities fraud resulted in the US Congress passing and enacting new legislation to prevent any other Kreuger from defrauding investors with worthless stocks and bonds. The Securities and Exchange Commission, the SEC, was established as a direct result of Kreuger's crimes. The world did not see another fraud as cunning and well-crafted until Enron imploded in 2001, having used many of Kreuger's techniques.

12 Bottles You Say? Not Interested
John Pemberton—Asa Candler— Ernest Woodruff

There are some success stories that are bigger than just one person. Three men with vastly different talents, within a short period of time, created an enterprise so successful and so enormous that even today it is recognized in virtually every corner of the globe. The Coca-Cola Company could not have been founded without the chemistry of John Pemberton, the marketing promotion of Asa Candler, and the cunning business drive of Ernest Woodruff.

The first player in this three-act play is Doc John Pemberton. Pemberton was a local Atlanta pharmacist and a chemist. Like many of his peers at the time, he made his living concocting remedies for people's ailments. A little alcohol, a little cocaine, a little caffeine, a little morphine, and *voila!* an elixir. The problem was that by the late 1800s, the government had passed temperance legislation that made Pemberton's newest creation, French Wine Cola, a hard sell.

Pemberton then started to think about creating a different product. He wanted something that he could sell to the masses, so alcohol was ruled out as an ingredient. Seeing the growing popularity of coffee, Pemberton saw a possible new direction.

Coffee was very popular in the winter but not as popular in the hot humid Atlanta summer. So he decided to make a cold summer beverage using some of the same ingredients in coffee.

Pemberton set up a three-legged kettle in his backyard and began the process of brewing this new beverage. He began with water, sugar, cocaine, caffeine, and a "little of this and a little of that." The last ingredient he added was caramel coloring. This was added in order to mimic the color of coffee and to hide any unexpected ingredients that may have dropped into the kettle. After all, this was an outdoor experiment. The coloring of products or the placing of them into dark-colored jars would hide any impurities and camouflage any damaged goods. This was an accepted practice in those days.

One of Pemberton's main partners in the new enterprise was Frank Robinson, a bookkeeper from Iowa. It was Robinson who gave the drink its name as well as the distinctive script trademark that is still in use today. The name Coca-Cola was chosen to announce to the public the two main "pick-me-up" ingredients of the product: the coca leaf and the kola nut. Interestingly enough, the temperance legislation did not ban or restrict the use of cocaine or caffeine.

Pemberton's first sales stop was the soda fountain of Jacobs' Pharmacy. As far as anyone can attest, the addition of carbonated water to the syrup may have not been Pemberton's idea but rather that of the soda jerk at Jacobs'. Carbonated water was known as a cure for ailments. The first-year sales for Coca-Cola were only fifty dollars. This resulted in a net loss to Pemberton and his investors. The second year was better, but not the huge success they had hoped for.

With Atlanta's repeal of the temperance act a mere one year after it was passed, Pemberton was able to increase the distribution of his French Wine Cola. This caused Pemberton to lose interest in Coca-Cola. Without his partners' knowledge, he sold the rights to Coca-Cola. He actually managed to sell the exclusive rights to

Coca-Cola more than four times, which included giving the rights to his alcoholic son.

Asa Candler was introduced to Coca-Cola through an attorney who was handling the legal complaints from Pemberton's original investors. At first, Candler was not interested. But with a little more persuading and prodding, Candler saw the possibilities. He bought the rights for a grand total of $2,300. Candler was now the owner of the exclusive rights to the handwritten formula, which included a three-legged brass kettle and the Coca-Cola name.

Candler incorporated this new venture as the Coca-Cola Company in 1888. But as you may recall, Pemberton had transferred the rights to Coca-Cola four other times. So for a brief time, Candler tried to market the drink under two alternative names: Yum Yom and Koka. Neither one caught on. Candler's only choice was to buy out and settle with the other parties.

Shortly after buying the rights to Coca-Cola, Asa Candler hired Frank Robinson. Candler, being a strict Southern Methodist, was not happy with the taste of Coca-Cola, nor the fact that it contained extract from the coca leaf that produced cocaine. To remedy these drawbacks, Asa and Frank set out to adjust the formula. The two wanted a more widely accepted taste, while trying to rid the formula of the coca leaf. The problem was that by eliminating the coca leaf, they would need to change the name of the product because it would no longer have the ingredient advertised in the name.

As the dangers of cocaine began to emerge, Candler was eager to remove it from Coca-Cola. The federal government was also after him to remove it. Candler went so far as to hire a cocaine manufacturer to come up with something from the coca leaf that would allow him to keep it in his drink but would not be detectable as cocaine. The fight with the federal government over cocaine eventually ended in the Supreme Court, where the justices ruled that a trade name didn't have to reflect the ingredients in a product.

Candler was a marketing genius. Along with Robinson, he created coupon promotions, colorful trade materials, and an entire list of products that would have the Coca-Cola name. He created trays, signs, and awnings, all promoting the drink that Robinson promoted as "delicious and refreshing."

Candler then made what appeared to be one of the greatest business blunders of all time: he made an exclusive deal with two men from Tennessee, Benjamin F. Thomas and Joseph B. Whitehead, to bottle Coca-Cola. At first, Candler was not interested in their idea. But Thomas and Whitehead were very persuasive. They convinced Candler to give them a license to sell Coca-Cola in bottles. Candler created a handwritten document that became a binding agreement for the sum of one dollar. This agreement gave Thomas and Whitehead the rights to use the Coca-Cola name on the bottles. They were able to buy the syrup at a fixed cost.

At first glance, this might seem like the dumbest business decision of the decade. After all, Coca-Cola was quickly becoming a household name. Sales were soaring, and Candler was making millions. But to Candler's way of thinking, the bottling process was nothing but trouble. Bottling the drink required setting up factories across the country. That required investing in a lot of equipment. The bottles themselves had to be collected and sanitized after each use, which cost even more money. Furthermore, many bottles were still being sealed with corks, and there was the possibility of an explosion from the pressure of the carbonation. The bottle cap as we know it today had only just been invented and was not yet widely used. Candler believed the best way to conduct the business was to mix a collection of ingredients and ship it to users who could put it in a container of their choice. To Candler's way of thinking, he was getting the better part of the deal with zero risk. All he had to do was provide the ingredients. He let the gentlemen from Tennessee worry about the bottles and the factories. This deal came back to haunt Coca-Cola several years later.

Coca-Cola's success started Candler thinking about his retirement. He was also worried about the longevity of Coca-Cola.

Would the government attack one of the ingredients? Would it fall from favor with the public, like so many other novelty drinks? Would a new competitor arrive on the scene? Candler was ready to cash out. He decided to put the Coca-Cola Company up for sale. He was willing to sell it to anyone except Ernest Woodruff, the local bank president of the Trust Company of Georgia. Woodruff, however, wanted to get his hands on the Coca-Cola Company. Woodruff already owned the largest bank in town as well as a number of other large corporations, so why not Coca-Cola?

Knowing he couldn't make an offer directly to Candler, Woodruff hired a New York firm to act as his "straw man" and put in an offer to buy the company. After much negotiation, they settled on a sale price of $20 million. The funds were secretly transferred. The Trust Company of Georgia was now the owner of the Coca-Cola Company.

With much fanfare, Woodruff went to the New York office of Coca-Cola and was photographed receiving the formula for Coca-Cola from the company safe. Then he traveled back to Atlanta, where he placed the secret formula in the safe at the Trust Company of Georgia. That is where it remains today. This was Woodruff's first promotional act for the Coca-Cola Company. The formula is so secretive, it must be locked up in a vault.

Woodruff was relentless in growing the company. Through expanded marketing and some questionable business tactics used to crush the completion, Coca-Cola kept growing. The only part of Coca-Cola that he didn't control was the bottling portion. In fact, with the rise in sugar prices, Coca-Cola was losing money on the shipments to bottlers under Candler's handwritten contract. Woodruff was determined to break the contract. Breaking a handwritten contract that was hastily written might have been easy, but the problem was that the two men who held the rights had sold the franchising rights to others for use under their own contract. By this time, the two men had passed away. Nevertheless, Woodruff was determined. After much negotiation and, some may say, threats to the heirs of the agreement, Woodruff gained the control he needed.

Woodruff was then able to create a uniform bottling program. What he needed was a bottle so distinctive that it would be immediately recognizable anywhere or anytime. Most importantly, the bottle needed to be recognized in the dark or if it were broken. At the turn of the century, bottles of cold drinks were placed in barrels of ice at general stores. When the ice melted, the bottles sank to the bottom of the barrel. Customers had to feel around for what they wanted. It was easy to pull up a competitor's drink if all the bottles felt the same.

Enter the Root Glass Company of Terra Haute, Indiana. The Root family was one of the early bottlers of Coca-Cola. Woodruff told Root that he wanted to create a distinctive bottle that no one could mistake for a competitor's beverage. Chapman Root turned the project over to his chief superintendent, T. Clyde Edwards, and his glass designer, Earl Dean. Edwards and Dean started their design process by taking a trip to the Emeline Fairbanks Memorial Library to research ideas for a distinctive Coca-Cola bottle. They started by looking up pictures of the ingredients used in mixing Coca-Cola. When they found a picture of a cocoa pod, they had a direction. They felt the distinctive ribs of the cocoa pod were easily recognizable and would be unique in feel if someone had his eyes closed or reached blindly into a barrel of cold icy water. The original prototype—which, like the cocoa pod, had a bulging rib center—was rejected. It was too unstable for the conveyor belts that ran the bottling line. The next design, which widened the bottom and narrowed the center, was patented. It was put into universal production. That single bottle design made millions for the Root family. Dean, the head designer, was rewarded with an offer of a $5,000 bonus or a job for life. He took the job for life.

To this day, the famous Coca-Cola recipe resides in the vault where Ernest Woodruff originally placed it. The bank that Ernest Woodruff once owned is now called SunTrust. It is still one of the largest shareholders of Coca-Cola stock, receiving over $50 million a year in annual dividends.

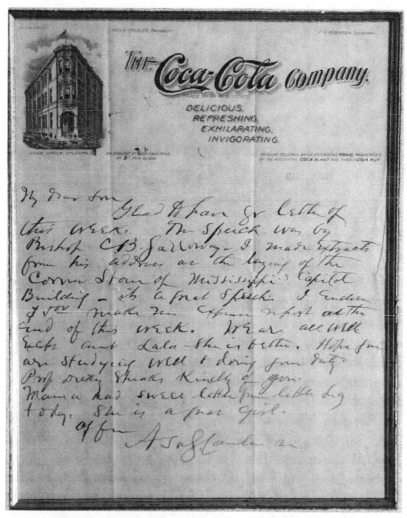

Document signed by Asa Chandler on Coca Cola letterhead.
Notice the building in the top left. Chandler built the building
and commented it was so large Coca Cola would never need
more space.

13 What a Circus!
John Ringling

The circus has been around for centuries. The Romans used the circus to display animals and to perform in front of audiences while riding chariots. Today, there are even groups called "the circus" that have acrobats and dancers performing and don't use animals at all, as well as the more traditional circus groups of clowns, acrobats, and animals under "the big top." There are many circus shows still touring, and some are quite successful. But none can compare to the shows performed by the Ringling Bros. and Barnum & Bailey Circus. That is the granddaddy of them all.

Ringling Bros. and Barnum & Bailey is, by far, the oldest operating circus in the United States. The credit for its lasting so long has to be given to the five Ringling brothers: Alfred, Albert, Charles, John, and Otto. The brothers were not from a circus family or even a performing family. They were just five brothers who had seen a circus in their hometown and said, "We can do that."

At first, their circus was no more than the brothers trying to do tricks, acrobatics, and comedy. The secret to their lasting success in the early years was their adherence to a tight budget and their reputation for honesty and fair dealings.

The Ringling brothers were diligent about putting all of their profits from the early days back into the show or into the bank "for a rainy day." A traveling circus was very labor-intensive and very costly to maintain. Moving from town to town took enormous coordination, a huge amount of supplies, and a lot of money. Many a circus of the day didn't survive because of the enormous cost of set-up and tear-down from town to town, across the country. Because the Ringling brothers saved their money, they were in a perfect position to add to their young circus by buying the assets of failing competitors. The five brothers trusted each other. They worked together as a team to assure a smoothly run operation.

John Ringling was the most famous of the brothers. He sang and clowned around in the shows during the early years. As the enterprise grew, his gregarious personality transformed him into the front man for the circus.

John visited many cities and towns months in advance in order to secure the space and make the necessary arrangements for the circus appearances. Food and supplies were needed to feed the virtual army of support staff and performers as well as the vast menagerie of animals who entered the "big top" on show day.

By the early 1900s, the Ringlings' circus had over one hundred private rail cars. They were crammed with supplies and people traveling across the nation, stopping in small towns and big cities alike. They were unloading one day and packing up and moving out the next. They became expert at moving vast amounts of people, supplies, and animals. It was the way they moved everything so efficiently that caught the eye of the US military during World War I.

The Ringling brothers were not only moving a hundred rail cars loaded with animals, supplies, tents, and performers, but they were also doing it at lightning speed, a technique the US Army was keen to learn. The Ringlings' methods were so synchronized that the military contracted with the brothers to train army supply officers on how to efficiently and quickly load and unload army supply trains under the conditions they might encounter during the war.

By 1920, the Ringling Brothers Circus was still not the biggest or most recognized circus in the country. That title belonged to Barnum & Bailey. Although Barnum & Bailey was the largest and most famous circus, the Ringling Brothers Circus was the most profitable and successful.

The Ringling brothers entered the circus business at the same time as P. T. Barnum, who had not yet teamed with Bailey. The Barnum & Bailey Circus floundered under mismanagement after the death of both Barnum in 1891 and James Bailey in 1906.

By 1907, the Bailey heirs sold out to the Ringling brothers, thereby making them one of the largest circus operators in the world. Along with the sale, the brothers also received the famous Buffalo Bill's Wild West Show that Barnum had purchased years earlier and was virtually debt-free.

After the purchase of the Barnum & Bailey Circus in 1907, the Ringling brothers chose to operate both circuses separately. There were two different touring companies, each going to different towns and cities.

With the unexpected death of Otto Ringling in 1911, followed by the deaths of Al Ringling in 1916 and Alf Ringling in 1919, the remaining brothers John and Charles decided it was too challenging to run two separate touring troupes. In 1919, the brothers merged the two companies to form the famous Ringling Bros. and Barnum & Bailey's Greatest Show on Earth.

The Ringling Bros. and Barnum & Bailey Circus, along with other touring groups that John and Charles owned, were making huge sums of money. John invested in stocks, railroads, mining, and real estate. He was quickly becoming one of the richest men in the world. It was his idea to move the circus out of its winter quarters in Wisconsin, where the brothers were from, to land that he had purchased in Sarasota, Florida.

John's years in Sarasota were responsible for transforming a small west-coast Florida town into a vacation paradise. He bought large tracts of land where he developed hotels, houses, shops, government buildings, and bridges. There was only one person who owned more developed land there. That was Henry Flagler, a Standard Oil partner.

John built his own home on the shores of Sarasota Bay. It was, by far, one of the finest and most unique mansions built in America during the end of the gilded age. It was built in a Venetian gothic style, reminiscent of the doge's palace in Venice.

John's great and expanding wealth allowed him to take up art collecting. He purchased so many collections of Baroque art while traveling that he had to build a museum on the grounds of his Sarasota home in which to keep them. The museum was large enough to house the collection of a small city. It served as a way for John Ringling to showcase his many wall-sized paintings by such masters as Rubens, van Dyck, Velázquez, Titian, Tintoretto, and Veronese, as well as tapestries and bronze statues.

With the passing of his brother Charles in 1926, John was in firm control of the circus. John's success in Sarasota real estate, railroads, and the stock market convinced him that he was ready for his next big act. He wanted to purchase his largest competitor, the American Circus Corporation. By combining the Ringling circus with the American Circus, Ringling would have the largest circus operating in the United States. He would control virtually every traveling circus that performed around the country.

John personally paid $1.7 million cash to buy the American Circus. He planned to take the company public in a stock offering the following year. Unfortunately, John's timing was off. On October 29, 1929, the stock market crashed. John could only watch as his wealth evaporated. The assets that once had great value, like railroads and real estate, were now a cash drain. Not in keeping with his brother's discipline of thrift and savings, John had huge debts. He was not able to pay his creditors.

In 1932, his Nephew and sisters voted to remove him from the circus that he had worked so hard to build. This was devastating to him. But despite his catastrophic financial losses, John, with the help of his nephew John Ringling North, was able to keep and maintain his home and museum in Sarasota, Florida.

Even though John Ringling lost control of the circus, he received a modest salary on which to live. It was, again, John Ringling North, his nephew, who helped him in his final years. North also worked tirelessly after John's death to settle his uncle's accounts. John Ringling, the last of the famous Ringling brothers, died on December 2, 1936. In his will, John bequeathed his home, Ca' d'Zan (House of John), and his museum to the state of Florida. Both were to be used for educational purposes.

The story doesn't end there. For another nine years—this was fifteen years after the great stock-market crash that wiped John Ringling out—his Ringling real-estate assets, which John Ringling North was able to keep from creditors, recovered enough in value to settle all of the creditors' claims. With the clearing of all of John Ringling's debts, the State of Florida was finally able to take possession of Ringling's estate and museum. John Ringling North was able to take control of his uncle's famous and, once again, highly successful circus to assure that a Ringling would continue the Greatest Show on Earth.

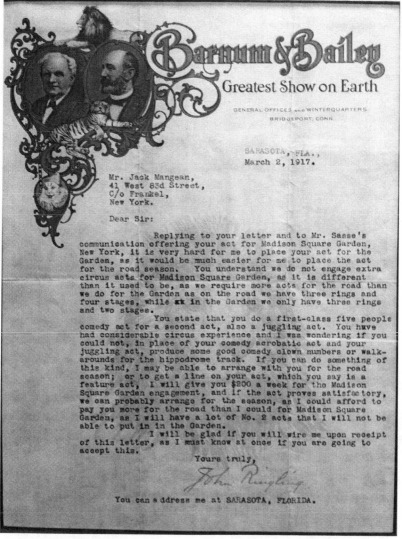

Ornate document signed by John Ringling on Barnum and Bailey letterhead. Ringling brothers operated many circuses under different names which toured the country. This allowed them to enter towns with a fresh new show. They eventually merge Barnum and Bailey with Ringling Brothers circus in 1919

14 Special Delivery: Larry Hillblom

Have you ever heard that some stories are so unbelievable "you just can't make this stuff up"? Larry Hillblom's life is one such story. He grew up on a farm in central California and subsequently "made it" in the big city—not just one city, but many large and small cities around the world. Larry was labeled eccentrically brilliant by his family and friends, and he showed a knack for business and innovation at an early age.

After high school, Hillblom left the family farm to attend Reedley College. Then he went to California State University, Fresno, and eventually earned a law degree from Boalt Hall School of Law at the University of California, Berkeley.

In order to pay for school, Larry took out student loans and worked numerous jobs. One such job was as clerk for the famous San Francisco attorney Melvin Belli, who was known as "The King of Torts." One of Hillblom's duties was to be a courier between San Francisco and Los Angeles. He caught the last flight of the day from SFO to LAX and returned to San Francisco on the first flight the next morning. He repeated these trips up to five times a week. He did this for four years until another young entrepreneur, Fred Smith, started a delivery service known as Federal Express, which delivered packages overnight without a courier.

During his package runs, Hillblom had a brainstorm. He noticed that cargo ships bringing goods into US ports were slow in removing their cargo. This delay was caused by the laborious task of checking the shipping manifests and getting the goods processed through customs. Larry believed that if the shipper could get the shipping documents to the customs officials before the ship docked, the majority of the paperwork could be cleared before the ship reached port.

The year was 1969, and most people were not thinking globally. Larry Hillblom, on the other hand, could see the future, and that future included globalization. Hillblom figured there was a large market for a company in the document delivery business. Up to that time, the document-delivery business was controlled and protected by the post office. Larry had another brainstorm. His idea eventually broke the monopoly of one of the largest enterprises in the world, the United States Postal Service. Larry used the balance of his student-loan money to recruit two of his friends to help him run this new business: Adrian Dalsey and Robert Lynn. Together, they founded a company called DHL.

The first route they chose was San Francisco to Hawaii. The three men shared a 1969 Plymouth Duster that they drove around San Francisco picking up documents and stuffing them into their suitcases. They then rushed to the airport to book their flights. Because they were short on cash, the three men charged their tickets to the company's new American Express business card.

The company expanded rapidly. Before long, the partners found themselves in all the same sites as the US Postal Service. The postal service had the monopoly on delivering mail, and DHL was interfering with that monopoly. Hillblom welcomed the challenge. He more than welcomed it. He thrived on it. Hillblom and DHL eventually prevailed in court, winning the landmark case against the postal service that opened the door for the private-letter delivery business.

With the postal-service case behind him, Hillblom had another fight to win—this time with the FBI. Someone had tipped off the FBI about a string of couriers who were flying overseas with briefcases. The FBI was certain that DHL was into illegal activities. After an exhaustive investigation, nothing amiss was discovered. Even some of the FBI agents on the case became couriers on their days off.

With these legal battles behind him, Hillblom decided to expand. Hillblom had always been fascinated with the Asian Pacific market. That was to be the next expansion area. By the early 1970s, he had expanded to the Philippines, Japan, Hong Kong, Singapore, and Australia. Money was pouring in so quickly that Hillblom decided to buy out his partners and go it alone.

Hillblom was driven to open new territories. When Federal Express came on the scene with its package-delivery service, DHL was focused on international package shipments. Hillblom was so focused on the international market that he completely missed the domestic US market. DHL, by the end of the 1970s, was the dominant international player in package and document delivery services. By the time Hillblom entered the US market, he was playing catch-up with UPS and Federal Express. DHL may have been number-one internationally, but it was a distant third in the United States.

In the 1980s, Hillblom moved from the United States to the island of Saipan, which he made his home. It was on Saipan that the DHL story ends, and the Larry Hillblom story begins.

Although Hillblom owned one of the world's largest air-shipment companies and a large fleet of cargo jets, he was enamored with vintage aircraft. He liked collecting them, fixing them, and flying them. But he didn't bother to get a pilot's license.

Hillblom's antique-aircraft obsession moved front and center in his life and, eventually, in his death. It was either his lack of pilot training, his daredevil attitude, or his penchant for very old aircraft that was the cause of his demise. After walking away from several crashes that should have killed this modern-day Howard Hughes, he finally met his end on May 21, 1995. On a flight from Pagan Island to Saipan, his vintage seaplane crashed into the

Pacific. The bodies of the copilot and that of a fellow passenger were found. Hillblom's body was never recovered.

Before Hillblom's untimely death, he had been involved in two other crashes. One of the crashes landed him in the medical center at the University of California, San Francisco, where he had reconstructive surgery to repair damage to his face. While recuperating, he told the entire staff that he was so grateful for their care that, when he died, he was going to leave the hospital $100 million. As it turned out, the actual amount that Hillblom left the UCSF Medical Center was $3 million. He left the rest of his money to the university itself. Since Hillblom had never married and had no children that he knew of, he didn't think it necessary to include a "disinheritance clause" in the 1982 will.

After Hillblom's death, his house in Saipan was scrubbed clean with muriatic acid. All of his clothes and possessions were buried. It didn't seem significant then. However, it later played a part in a long battle for his estate, which included almost every lawyer in Saipan and even many in the United States. As it happened, Hillblom had a darker side.

It was discovered that Hillblom's choice to move to Saipan was not to be close to his worldwide organization, but so he could jump from island to island looking for sex. It seems that Hillblom had a penchant for unprotected sex with young girls. He frequented bars and clubs throughout the Pacific. He offered bartenders and prostitutes money to set him up with very young and preteen virgins. What Hillblom didn't know at the time, or perhaps just didn't care about, was the fact that he might have been fathering children with many of these child liaisons. As it turned out, that is just what happened. When Hillblom died, young mothers from all around Southeast Asia stepped forward claiming that their children were heirs to Hillblom's $600 million estate.

Without Hillblom's body, it was difficult to prove these claims. Searching his house for DNA was worthless since it had been scrubbed clean with a muriatic acid solution. Digging up his clothes would prove nothing either. Remarkably, it was discovered that the UCSF Medical Center still had a mole that had been removed from Hillblom several years earlier. At first this was considered great news for the defense attorneys. But they soon found out that this evidence belonged to Hillblom's mother, who was still alive.

The defense tried everything. Its last gasp was to collect the DNA from all the children who claimed to belong to Hillblom in order to see if any of them had a common father. Unfortunately, this was not convincing proof for the Saipan courts. After some persistence, the defense attorneys for the children persuaded Hillblom's mother to supply DNA. It didn't come cheap. They had to give her $1 million and buy her a villa in France. They got the DNA, and that did the trick. It was ultimately determined that one Vietnamese child, two Filipino children, and one child from Palau were all fathered by Hillblom.

Hillblom, the man who challenged the US Postal Service and won, left no heirs that he was aware of or cared to acknowledge— but ended up with a forced court settlement for his children. The settlement was a flat payment of $90 million to each child, which added up to $360 million. The balance of his estate, $240 million, went to the Hillblom Foundation to fund medical research at the University of California, San Francisco.

15 You Have to Give Him Credit: Lewis Tappan

Lewis Tappan was brought up in a strict Calvinist home. He was deeply influenced by his devoted parents. At a young age, he started working in the family dry-goods business. This lasted until he reached age sixteen, at which time he set out on his own to establish a similar business. Lewis had his first lucky business break when the war broke out between America and the British in 1812.

Lewis was sitting on a stockpile of supplies when they suddenly rose in value. Thus, he was able to sell his wares at considerably more than he paid for them, and he made a tidy profit. Lewis even made enough money, so it seemed, to loan $75,000 to his brother Arthur to start a dry-goods business.

But Lewis's success didn't last long. Arthur, on the other hand, found tremendous success in the trading and dry-goods business in New York City. Because of some bad decisions, Lewis lost most of his previous earnings. In need of work, he headed to New York City to join his brother Arthur in the silk-trading business.

It was there that Lewis and Arthur became active abolitionists who fought to end slavery. The rest of the Tappan family, strict Calvinists all, were against Lewis's extreme and radical ideas. Lewis, Arthur, and Samuel F. B. Morse established the *Journal of Commerce.* This was a weekly magazine that focused on trade topics. They also helped organize the American Colonization Society. The society's goal was to send free blacks back to Africa, their rightful homeland. The problem was that many of the blacks of the time were actually born in the United States and had no knowledge or memory of Africa.

The society, under Lewis's leadership, did succeed in repatriating a Mississippi slave by the name of Abd-al-Rahman Ibrahima. The brothers hoped that repatriating Abd-al-Rahman Ibrahima would further their goal of freeing the slaves and returning them to Africa. In doing so, they thought that these former slaves would be grateful and in turn would help the Tappan brothers establish trade with Africa. Unfortunately, Abd-al-Rahman Ibrahima died shortly after he arrived in Africa.

The brothers soon realized that neither of their goals could be accomplished by the American Colonization Society. Both Lewis and his brother Arthur became frustrated and disappointed with the lack of progress. They decided to leave the American Colonization Society to pursue other methods directed at freeing the slaves in America.

After their departure from the American Colonization Society, Lewis, Arthur, their friend William Garrison, and others joined in establishing the American Anti-Slavery Society. Again, their views were seen as extreme. Lewis and Arthur advocated intermarriage between the races. Lewis believed that marriage between blacks and whites would lead to a race of "copper skins," and the divide over the races would naturally end.

Lewis established Anti-Slavery Societies throughout the state of New York. They began a mail campaign throughout the nation that generated sympathy for the cause—and even more importantly, financial support. Through the organization, in 1835, Lewis established Oberlin College in Ohio. The college was open to men and women of all races. However, as the organization grew, it began to splinter. When the society elected a woman to serve on the business committee and took up the cause of women's rights, Lewis resigned.

As enlightened as the Tappan's were to the horrors of slavery, they were still strict conservative Christian men who opposed women serving in any public capacity. The brothers broke away from the Anti-Slavery Society and started their own splinter group, the American and Foreign Anti-Slavery Society.

In 1839, when the slave ship *Amistad* sailed into New York Harbor carrying forty-nine slaves from Africa, Lewis saw it as a guiding moment to advance the cause of the abolitionists. The ship was controlled by a group of slaves who had successfully rebelled against their captors and seized control of the ship off the coast of Cuba. The slaves were under the impression they were sailing back to Africa. Instead, the two men the slaves had spared had sailed them not east to Africa but north to New York. While the *Amistad* was anchored off the coast of New York to gather fresh supplies of food and water, the naval ship USS *Washington* spotted it and recaptured it. The captain of the *Washington*, hoping to profit from the cargo, escorted the ship not to a port in New York but to a port in Connecticut, where slave ownership was still legal. He hoped that the courts would award him salvage rights, which would allow him to sell the remaining slaves.

Lewis and his organization entered the case hoping to gain the release of the slaves and public sympathy for the slaves' plight. Lewis organized a separate group he called the *Amistad* Committee that was in charge of raising money for the defense of the captured Africans.

Lewis and his brother used their magazine, the *Journal of Commerce*, to sway popular support for the slaves, who were incarcerated in a Connecticut jail. When the trial began, the slaves found themselves up against the interest of Spain, the ship's captain, the captain of the *Washington*, and the US government. All wanted a piece of the cargo. Martin van Buren, the president of the United States, was so interested in seeing the slaves returned to Spain that he ordered a ship to stand by off the coast of

Connecticut to be ready to transport the slaves back when the trial ended. This decision was made to thwart any appeal should the slaves petition a higher court.

To everyone's surprise, the slaves did, in fact, win their freedom. The lower court ruled that the captive slaves were not in fact slaves, but were free Africans who had been kidnapped against their will and loaded aboard the *Amistad* illegally. Immediately following the ruling, the US attorney general appealed the order to the Supreme Court.

The captives of the *Amistad* received the news that they were free and had the right to be returned to Africa should they choose to go. When the captives attained their freedom, it was Lewis who moved the thirty-five surviving black men and boys, and three girls, to the village of Farmingdale, Connecticut, which was Grand Central on the Underground Railroad. There they learned English and were converted to Christianity while they waited for the *Amistad* Committee to raise funds for their return trip to Africa, which was accomplished in 1842.

None of these actions went unnoticed. The brothers' mailings fired up the south. Southern Democrats accused them of trying to divide the union. In New York, where they had a thriving dry-goods store and silk-import business, there was rioting in the streets. Only Arthur's shotgun kept the mob from getting into the store and dragging the occupants into the street to be hanged. Lewis's home was not as safe. The angry mob that was unable to storm the store went to Lewis's house. They threw his furniture in the street and set the house on fire.

The brothers' successful silk-trade business collapsed. Sales fell off at the New York dry-goods store because of boycotts by Southern buyers and Northern slave supporters. Things turned especially difficult during the panic of 1837, which brought about a five-year depression and caused six hundred banks to collapse. Unemployment soared.

Lewis had always believed in dealing in cash to buy and sell goods. So he was surprised when he found out that his brother,

Arthur, had purchased over $1 million in goods on credit. Now he could not pay for the goods, nor could he extend credit to customers who could not pay cash for their purchases. Arthur struggled with the debt. He appealed to his creditors for some time to work off his balance. He assured everyone they would be paid for all past purchases, including interest on the debt. Lewis wrote to a friend that the credit system he was using was ruinous.

In order to move product, the brothers found it was still necessary to extend credit for sales. There just weren't enough greenbacks or gold around to conduct commerce transactions for cash and increase sales. But there had to be someone they could sell to who would assure they would get paid back. Their business sold not only to companies in New York City but also to businesses in other states.

Lewis had an idea. He started a ledger and entered anything and everything he could find out about the people he sold to. Did they gamble? Drink? Have assets? Did they have an honest reputation? He traveled around the streets and inquired about the businesses and the men who ran them, and he wrote down what he heard. The information in Lewis's book was instrumental in allowing his brother's dry-goods business to sell on credit and get paid promptly.

Lewis kept busy hiring correspondents who could collect information about businesses. They forwarded their findings to Lewis in New York. Most correspondents were his fellow abolitionists around the country. The success brought about by selling on credit successfully allowed Arthur to pay off all his creditors within eighteen months at an interest rate of 15 percent.

Before long, other business owners came into Arthur's dry-goods store and inquired of Lewis who they might sell to. At first, Lewis gave them the information for free. Most of the people asking were his abolitionist friends. He saw it as a way of thanking them for their support. As his files grew, Lewis soon recognized that he could actually make a business out of selling the information.

Lewis informed Arthur that he was going out on his own to start a credit-reporting service. Arthur didn't think much of the idea. He predicted that Lewis would be back working at the store within months.

Lewis established the Mercantile Agency in the summer of 1841. It was the first full credit-reporting agency in the world. In order to break even, Lewis needed to sign one hundred subscribers in the first year. At the beginning, most businesses saw what Tappan was doing as a colossal invasion of privacy. After five months, Tappan had signed less then eleven subscribers. But he still believed in his business idea. He persevered, lowered his prices, and knocked on more doors. The first year ended with a loss. He had only forty clients, less than half of what he had projected. Eventually, though, his perseverance paid off. By 1844, he had two hundred and eighty clients. He had branches in Boston, Baltimore, and Philadelphia.

With the American economy expanding again, there was a migration west and a great need for credit information. Most businesses still relied on letters of recommendation from friends, clergy, or other references. The problem with that method was trying to verify the information. How would the recipient know if the letter was real or the person writing it was worthy of giving a recommendation? Lewis's system solved those problems.

As the business grew, more and more correspondents were hired. To help manage the business, Lewis took on Benjamin Douglass as the chief clerk. This allowed Lewis more time to hire correspondents and expand the Mercantile Agency to other areas. By 1851, ten years after Lewis started the agency, Mercantile had seven hundred subscribers in New York alone. It also had two thousand correspondents throughout the country sending back information to the offices.

One correspondent wrote of Huntington, Hopkins, Stanford, and Crocker—"The Associates" who founded the Central Pacific

Railroad—"They are making money fast." Many famous names were mercantile-agency correspondents. Presidents Ulysses S Grant, Grover Cleveland, William McKinley, and Abraham Lincoln were all correspondents at one time.

Lincoln wrote in one of his reports that a grocer "had a rat hole that would bear looking into." Grant noted that a young lawyer had a "barrel and a board for a desk and a nice young wife." He reckoned his compassion for the law made him a good risk.

Benjamin Douglass was doing a fine job running the Mercantile Agency. In 1851, Lewis was ready to hand over the reins of the company to Douglass and make him a partner. Lewis's brother Arthur objected. To settle the dispute, Lewis offered to buy his brother's share, thereby giving Lewis full control of the company and allowing him to turn the company over to Douglass and to Douglass's brother-in-law, Robert Dun. By 1859, Douglass was ready to retire, leaving Dun in full control of the company.

Dun set out to make changes to the company. The first was to change the name of the company to R. G. Dun & Company. Dun's vision was to do a statistical analysis of a company and not to rely as much on the opinions and writings of the correspondents. This made it easier for subscribers to understand the asset value and risk associated with a particular borrower. Under Dun, the company grew throughout the United States and expanded internationally.

Dun's largest competitor in the field was John Bradstreet. Bradstreet started his reporting agency, the Bradstreet Company, in Cincinnati in 1849.

By 1855, Bradstreet had moved to New York and was ready to take on the Mercantile Agency directly. The Bradstreet Company's service differed from the service offered by the Mercantile Agency.

Subscribers had to go to a Mercantile company office or to a correspondent to get a credit rating. The Bradstreet Company published its credit information in book form that was supplied to its subscribers. Bradstreet also pioneered the credit rating that was assigned to a company. A Bradstreet subscriber could look up a company in one book and use another book to decipher the codes.

By 1859, when Dun took over the Mercantile Company, he found that John Bradstreet was making strong inroads with his subscriber base. Subscribers found Bradstreet's method of sending books to a client's place of business much more convenient than sending someone to a Mercantile office.

The Mercantile Agency had always been hesitant to put information in written form. They didn't want to let it leave the office. But with Bradstreet's success, Dun could no longer hold out. He found himself forced to compete directly with John Bradstreet by publishing his ratings. Dun published his own volume, called the Dun's Book. His book required a lock and key to keep the reports from the prying eyes of nonsubscribers.

It was inevitable that the two largest credit-reporting agencies would one day merge. That day came in 1933 during the height of the Depression. Under the leadership of R. G. Dun and CEO Arthur Whiteside, R. G. Dun and The Bradstreet Company merged. This created the international powerhouse Dun & Bradstreet.

16 Damn, Missed the Boat Again: Milton Hershey

As confectioners go, there is none more famous than Milton Hershey. For more than one hundred years, his chocolate bar has been consistently one of the best-selling candies in history. No other candy bar has matched the Hershey Bar's longevity. Oddly enough, Hershey wasn't always in the chocolate business. He started his business career as a printer's apprentice. But he hated the printing business. One day he let his hat fall into a press in the hopes of getting fired. It worked.

Hershey's next career move landed him in the candy business. He fell in love with the business when he went to work as an apprentice for a small candy-maker in Lancaster, Pennsylvania. Hershey enjoyed making candy. He found it very rewarding. His love of making candy instilled in him the desire to become his own boss and start his own candy company.

Hershey trained in Lancaster for four years before he decided it was time to form his own candy company. He did not want to be in competition with his former boss, so staying in Lancaster was out of the question. His choice for the perfect place to start his career as a candy-company owner was Philadelphia. With help from his mother, who was only of modest means herself, he started his new company.

After six years of hard work, Hershey's candy company was a complete failure. But this failure did not deter Hershey. This was the business he wanted to be in, and he believed that success would be his if he just found the right product. It was then that Hershey heard about a new process for making caramels. He found the process intriguing. He headed west to Denver to work for the company that was making the chewy candy. The "new" recipe required the addition of milk.

With that experience under his belt and a recipe for a different type of caramel, Hershey headed back Pennsylvania to start a caramel company. Again, he didn't want to compete with the man who had trained him. So with his mother's help again, he set up his first shop in Chicago. Then he moved to New York. The company failed a second time.

In 1883, with his mother's encouragement, he went back to Lancaster to try again. He used his mother's kitchen to perfect his caramel recipe and start another candy company. The new company was named the Lancaster Caramel Company. This time it was an immediate success. (It is interesting to note that another young entrepreneur had tried and failed to start a company in other cities just four years earlier. He, too, finally found the success he was looking for in Lancaster. That young merchant was Frank W. Woolworth. (see Woolworth chapter 24)

Milton Hershey had outstanding success with the Lancaster Caramel Company. Within a few years, his caramel factory employed fourteen hundred workers. It shipped throughout the United States and across the seas to Europe. He was at the top of the candy business and was one of Lancaster's leading citizens. But Hershey wasn't done yet.

While visiting Chicago's Columbian exhibition in 1893, Hershey became fascinated with a German company's equipment that automated the process of making chocolate. Hershey ordered the equipment and had it installed at the Lancaster caramel factory. He used it to make a chocolate coating for a new line of caramel candies. Hershey immediately recognized this as a new market. In anticipation of a higher demand for this chocolate, he started a new division called the Hershey Chocolate Company.

The Hershey Chocolate Company produced a sweet dark chocolate for coating the caramels. They were sold in bulk to confectioners throughout the United States. Over time, Hershey became obsessed with creating and mass-producing milk chocolate in America. Up until then, the only manufacturers of milk chocolate in the world were the Swiss, and they were not interested in sharing their process with anyone.

If Hershey wanted to make milk chocolate, he was going to have to figure it out himself. Day after day, month after month, batch after ruined batch, Hershey experimented with mixes and cooking methods. Finally, through trial and error, he hit upon the correct combination of ingredients and an important method that allowed him to mass produce milk chocolate. What had once been an expensive luxury controlled by the Swiss was now available for a nickel in the form of a Hershey Bar that everyone could enjoy.

In 1900, with sales at the Hershey Chocolate Company growing and Hershey convinced that milk chocolate was the next growth product, he decided to sell the caramel company to focus on the mass production of milk chocolate. With the $1 million he received for the sale of the caramel division, Hershey bought forty thousand acres of undeveloped farmland north of Lancaster. There he established a state-of-the-art chocolate-manufacturing facility to make his new milk chocolate. Hershey chose the site so he would be close to large quantities of the fresh dairy milk needed to mass produce milk chocolate.

Hershey guessed right. Milk chocolate sales soared. The Hershey Bar quickly became the most popular candy bar in the country. Shortly after came the Hershey Kiss. The manufacturing of the Hershey Kiss was deafeningly noisy. Hundreds of women were employed to turn over pans used to form the little chocolate kisses. They then loosened them with the strike of a mallet. This went on until a simpler, quieter machine was finally installed.

Forty thousand acres of land, over sixty square miles, is a lot for just one factory, but Hershey wasn't interested in building just a factory. He was confident in the demand for Hershey chocolates and the growth of the company. He intuitively knew that this growth would require not only skilled workers but also happy workers. This would limit turnover and therefore ensure success.

Hershey decided to build a utopian industrial town to take care of his employees. This would ensure that he would have a skilled and happy workforce close to the factory. Most company towns of the day were little more than shantytowns. Hershey wanted his town to be the finest. So he built schools, houses, parks, auditoriums, shops, and civic buildings. He made sure that all of the buildings were of top quality. He also installed one of the finest trolley systems in the state, linking other towns so it would be easy for workers who did not live in his company town to arrive on time.

By the time the factory was finished in 1905 and turning out chocolate, it was a magnet for people who were leaving the farms and looking for work. The factory grew, and so did the town. In 1908, Hershey built a fine mansion for himself and his wife on a hill that overlooked the factory and the growing town of Hershey. He also built a fine brick house across the street from the chocolate factory for his biggest fan and earliest investor, his mother, Fanny. He visited her every day before he went home to his mansion on the hill.

With all the joy Milton Hershey brought to children with the nickel candy bar, he and his wife, Catherine, were not able to have children of their own. In 1909, their love for children drove Milton and Catherine to establish the Hershey Industrial School for Orphaned Boys. This was a true labor of love for the two philanthropists.

Catherine Hershey did not live to see the tremendous growth of the Hershey Company and the town she helped build. Nor did she see the many thousands of boys and, eventually, girls the

Hershey Trust educated. She passed away in 1915 after a long debilitating muscular illness. Milton Hershey was crushed.

Three years after his wife's death, in 1918, Hershey secretly transferred most of his wealth and his Hershey stock to the Hershey Trust to be held for the benefit of the industrial school that he and his wife loved so much. Hershey remarked that since he didn't have heirs of his own to inherit his fortune, the orphans of the United States would be his heirs.

From 1918 on, he stopped spending a lot of time in the town of Hershey and at the factory. He traveled for a time to Cuba, where he created another utopian industrial town. Throughout the 1920s, he poured millions of Hershey profit dollars into building a sugar refinery in Cuba. He surrounded the factory with a new town of fine houses, shops, parks, and another orphanage and school for boys.

Although Hershey did not spend the majority of his time in the United States, when he did return, he found it very lonely in the large mansion he had built. So in 1928, he decided to move into a small sitting room and bedroom on the second floor of the mansion. He turned the rest of the home into a country club for the citizens of Hershey. His favorite pastime was sitting in his two-room suite with Hershey's president, Bill Murrie, playing cards and talking about the factory.

With the crash of the stock market, the onset of the Great Depression, and the entire country in a state of shock, the town of Hershey was hardly affected at all. "It's now that a man with money should do something for the people," Hershey remarked. So he made sure that the people of Hershey were employed and all benefits and services were still provided.

To that end, he decided to expand the town for a third time. From 1929 to 1936, Hershey funded an array of multimillion dollar construction projects. He funded a $3 million community building that held a fifty-eight-bed hospital, dormitories for men, a swimming pool, recreational facilities, classrooms for the industrial school, a cafeteria, a public library, and theaters. All were built and dedicated at the height of the Depression in 1933. Hershey continued building well into the 1930s, adding a new Hershey Hotel, the Hershey Sports Arena, a $1.5 million addition to the Hershey Industrial School, and an amusement park on a thousand acres that included a ballroom, four golf courses, the state's largest swimming pool, and the country's largest zoo.

Hershey's legacy lives on to this day. The Hershey Trust still controls the majority of the Hershey Company stock. The profits still go to the Hershey Industrial School. It has been renamed the Milton Hershey School and is now open to low-income families and children with special needs.

In Hershey's time, orphan children lived on communal farms and attended classes to learn a trade. Today, the school provides housing, clothes, books, and education for K-12 children, free of charge. The Hershey Trust even pays the tuition for graduates who have the ability and desire to attend college. With the seemingly unlimited supply of Hershey money, the school boasts state-of-the-art facilities and a low 15:1 student-teacher ratio. All this is free of charge to children, compliments of Milton S. Hershey, the man who put his heart and soul into caring for people.

This incredible gift to the children of the United States might never have happened if it had not been for the illness of Mrs. Hershey. The year was 1912, and the Hersheys had just completed a European vacation. They were waiting in England for the ship to take them back to the states. Like other people of means, they were excited to sail on the most elegant ocean liner ever built—the legendary, unsinkable *Titanic*. Because of Mrs. Hershey's illness, Mr. Hershey canceled their voyage at the last minute. The Hershey Trust received its bequest in 1918, some six years after the sinking of the *Titanic*. Thus, as fate would have it, had the Hersheys been onboard the *Titanic* that fateful night, there might never have been a Hershey School.

17 Maybe Walking on the Moon Was Worth It: Philo Farnsworth

The story of the boy genius experimenting on the family farm and coming up with an invention that changed the world has been fictionalized in books, movies, and television. In the case of Philo Farnsworth, though, it isn't make believe. It is the real deal.

Philo did indeed grow up on a farm. He was born in 1906 to Lewis and Serena Farnsworth, Mormons living in a log cabin built by Lewis's father in Utah. When Philo was twelve, the family moved from the humble cabin to a farm in Rugby, Idaho. Philo's father worked the land and also managed to supplement his income by hauling freight with his horse-drawn carriage. It was on this farm that Philo became fascinated with, of all things, electronics.

When Philo moved into the new home, he found that the house had electric lights that were powered by a small generator. During the day, the generator managed to provide electric power for various types of farm equipment. This stand-alone power generator seemed like magic to him.

While exploring his new surroundings, Philo stumbled on a stash of technology magazines in the attic. It was this discovery, and the fact that he had already seen what technology could do, that really sparked his interest. Technology, as it turned out, was something for which he had an aptitude. Day after day, he climbed into the attic. He used the electric light provided by the farm's generator to read the old journals that described the new exciting inventions of the day. He was hooked. It wasn't long before Philo was knowledgeable enough about mechanics and engineering to be able to make repairs to the family generator when needed.

Philo made other discoveries on the farm as well. When he stumbled upon an old broken electric motor that had been discarded by the previous tenant, he repaired it by rewiring the armature and bringing it back to life. Philo installed the old motor on his mother's hand-crank washing machine and connected it to the home generator. This provided his mother with one of the earliest automatic washing machines.

Philo attended the local high school in Rigby. At fourteen, he already excelled in physics and chemistry. It was in his chemistry class that he first produced sketches and prototypes of electron tubes. This eventually played a pivotal role in his future place in history.

Philo was only sixteen when his parents moved back to Utah in 1922, but he stayed behind to work for the railroad. He wanted to earn enough money to attend Brigham Young University. Philo's desire to attend college had to be postponed when his father suddenly passed away. This left him to help support his mother, two sisters, and two brothers.

At eighteen, still hoping to attend college, Philo decided to join the navy. His intake test score was the second-highest of any recruit that year. When he learned that any discovery he made would be the property of the US government, though, he sought and received an honorable discharge.

After he left the navy, Philo joined his mother and siblings in running a boardinghouse on the second floor of their home in Provo, Utah. While in Provo, he developed a close friendship with Cliff Gardner. Cliff shared Philo's love of electronics. The two decided to take their love of electronics to Salt Lake City, Utah's largest city, and open a radio repair shop. The venture didn't last long. Shortly after it opened, the shop failed. Gardner decided to move back to Provo. Philo stayed in Salt Lake City to look for work through the University of Utah job-placement program. This is where he met Leslie Gorrell and George Everson, two San Francisco philanthropists who were in town to raise money for the community chest. The two were intrigued with Philo's experiments and drawings. They saw tremendous possibilities and profit in his work.

Everson was sure he could raise the money Farnsworth needed for his experiments back home in California. He suggested Philo relocate and open a laboratory in Los Angeles. With the backing of Everson and Gorrell, Philo moved to Los Angeles. He set up a laboratory to continue perfecting his designs.

When Philo arrived in Los Angeles, Everson and Gorrell suggested it was time for him to contact a lawyer and file patents on his designs. Philo's designs were presented and filed at the patent office on January 7, 1927. The decision to file on that date turned out to be a critical turning point in the upcoming battles.

With money running out in Los Angeles, George Everson, a San Francisco native, persuaded Crocker Bank to invest in a new entity. Crocker officials agreed to supply space in one of the bank-owned buildings in San Francisco. They gave $25,000 in return for a stake in the newly formed Television Laboratories Inc.

In the summer of 1927 Everson, Gorrell, and Farnsworth moved the laboratory from Los Angeles to San Francisco. When the stock market crashed in 1929, the officers at Crocker Bank were worried about their investment in Farnsworth's work. Over the past two years, they had poured an additional $45,000 into the venture, and they were still far from a commercial product. Only a year earlier, Farnsworth had invited the Crocker bankers to his laboratory to demonstrate how his camera, which he called an "image detector," could send an image to a cathode-ray tube on the other side of the room. During that demonstration at

202 Green Street, the camera not only picked up the rotating two-dimensional images on the table, but it also broadcast the movement of smoke that drifted up from his brother-in-law's cigarette. This was the first televised transmission of movement over the airwaves. It was done with an all-cathode tube. Today, there is a plaque placed at 202 Green Street to commemorate the first television broadcast.

One year later, the Crocker officials were again at Farnsworth's laboratory door. This time, they were not invited. They had had enough. They wanted the lab shut down, everyone fired, and the remaining assets sold. This was a threat that Farnsworth didn't appreciate. Before the situation escalated out of control, Everson stepped in to work out a compromise. After all, what would the bank sell if the lab shut down? The patents were in Farnsworth's name. Farnsworth and his group of engineers were sure they were close to having a commercial product. Before the Crocker Bank executives left the building, the group of MIT, Stanford, and Berkeley engineers who were working with Farnsworth all agreed to work for no pay as long as Crocker didn't pull the plug on Television Laboratories Inc.

By the time Farnsworth perfected his invention and was ready to debut the all-cathode-ray-tube method of transmitting images wirelessly over the air, there were twenty new television stations, using an old and inferior mechanical system, broadcasting some form of crude images.

The mechanical imaging method that was developed by Scottish inventor John Baird used a rotating disk with holes punched in it to turn the light on and off. This created an image similar to a flip book. The rotating disk was only capable of sending a maximum of forty-five lines to a television receiver. That gave the viewer a very grainy image. The consumer wasn't impressed. This crude image coming over the airwaves didn't excite the public.

Farnsworth's use of a vacuum tube changed all that. His system pulsed electrons in a vacuum at ten thousand times a second, allowing him to draw five hundred lines on his receiver. When John Baird saw Farnsworth's demonstration, he left the room. He knew his system was doomed.

Farnsworth's system is still in use today, although liquid crystal displays (LCD) are quickly replacing Farnsworth's cathode-ray tubes (CRT).

David Sarnoff, the president of RCA, had been interested in the concept of television for years. He was one of the early backers of the mechanical disk system. Sarnoff had been using RCA money to fund secret research to develop an alternative method of broadcasting a television signal for several years. After tens of thousands of dollars spent, his researchers still couldn't find an alternate solution. When Sarnoff read about the young genius from the farm who had managed to solve the problem of sending moving pictures through the air, he rushed to San Francisco to see it.

Sarnoff cleverly managed to get Philo to invite him to his laboratory in San Francisco. He was accompanied by the head RCA engineer. The two of them made detailed notes during their visit. Farnsworth was very proud of his accomplishment. He didn't mind explaining it to anyone who would listen. With these notes in hand, Sarnoff's engineers developed a competing technology that was based on Farnsworth's work. They then filed their own patents under the RCA name. Sarnoff turned around and instructed his lawyers to sue Farnsworth for patent infringement.

Farnsworth eventually won the battle with Sarnoff and RCA with the help of his old high-school teacher. His teacher had kept his own detailed notes from the young man's experiments, and he provided important testimony at the patent trial. Farnsworth prevailed and proved RCA had stolen the technology and invention.

RCA eventually had to pay $1 million to Farnsworth as well as a small royalty on some key camera components. Unfortunately, to Farnsworth's disappointment, the battle lasted so long against

RCA that he was shut out of the market. He eventually sold what was left of his company to International Telephone & Telegraph (ITT) and worked for that company in a basement laboratory.

While working for ITT, Philo went on to invent a number of breakthrough products, including a defense early-warning signal, a submarine detection device, radar calibration equipment, and the infrared telescope. His later work and experiments included nuclear fusion.

In the end, it was his television technology that would be best remembered. It was an invention that he became very disappointed with, and one he would not put in his own home. Philo saw television as a way to educate and bring news directly to the people, without a middleman to interpret it. To Farnsworth, it was a way to see and communicate with people and cultures in different and far-off lands. He believed that if people saw and understood others of different cultures, there would be no reason for war. He expected that television would be the first step toward world peace. He saw it not as a delivery system for sitcoms and the broadcasting of endless episodes of *Dragnet and Lassie* but of important news and communication.

In the end, he did have a small change of heart. On July 20, 1969, he sat and watched as his invention broadcast to the world the first images of Neil Armstrong and Buzz Aldren as they emerged from the Lunar Lander and planted the American flag on the moon's surface.

18 You Figure It Out: Powel Crosley Jr.

During the first half of the twentieth century, there was hardly a more famous name then Powel Crosley. Powel was the owner and founder of Crosley Corporation, which was located in the bustling city of Cincinnati. The company invented or developed many of the items taken for granted today like soap operas, ice-cube trays, radios, radio stations, and of all things, the shelves on refrigerator doors. Believe it or not, all of these were patentable. These were only a few of the many items that Crosley and his brother, Lowell, invented.

At the height of Powel's fame, he was compared to Henry Ford. The media dubbed him "the Henry Ford of Radio." Although Powel didn't invent the radio, he did mass produce it, just as Henry Ford did with the car. Both Crosley and Ford managed to continually drive down the price of the two most important inventions of their time.

Powel never intended to get into the radio business. He manufactured phonographs with his brother in a small cabinet shop he acquired. It was his son who set him on the path to the radio business. Honestly, Powel regarded the newly invented radio as a toy. When his son kept pestering him for one, he relented and took the boy down to the local appliance store to see about a purchase. When he arrived, he found that radios were selling for anywhere from $100 to $300. He thought that was way too much money for a toy.

Powel went to the local bookstore and bought a book on radios and how they worked. After a quick trip to a hardware store, Powel and his son built a nice radio for a fraction of the retail cost. Powel now saw a market and a way to expand his cabinet-shop business. Why not build more of these homemade radios and bring down prices? His first radio was the Crosley Pup. It sold for an introductory price of under ten dollars, which was a full 90 percent less than his nearest competitor.

At that price, Crosley was selling hundreds, thousands, then hundreds of thousands of radios. To continue to drive the sales of his radios, he quickly realized that he needed more programming for his listeners. In the 1920s, there were few radio stations and even fewer programs. Most stations were run by hobbyists and were of very low power. Crosley decided it was up to him to provide more programming so that the general population would have a reason to purchase his radios. Along the way, he became the leader in creating the broadcasting industry.

His first radio station was located on the top floor of his radio factory. The station initially lost money. Even he had to admit that his programming was spotty. Powel quickly realized he needed even more programs. The programs needed to be broadcast for longer periods of the day. They even needed a few advertisers to help pay the bills.

Thus, his stations gave many young artists their start. Names like Doris Day, Rosemary Clooney, and Fats Waller were first heard broadcasting from a Crosley station. His studios also gave the world the first radio drama series, which was sponsored by Proctor & Gamble, the largest soap manufacturer in the country. It was this association between the drama shows and Proctor & Gamble that resulted in the now familiar term "soap opera."

Soap operas and music were not the only things Crosley's WLW broadcasted. During the Great Depression, Powel had the opportunity to buy the Cincinnati Reds. Though he was not a baseball fan at the time, he nevertheless saw some commercial possibilities in owning the team.

Powel had invested in his own company over the years. When the stock market crashed, he was one of the fortunate ones who had a lot of cash to make purchases. Powel bought the team. His station was the first to broadcast a baseball game over the airwaves, play by play, for his listening audience.

The team lost money for the first few years. So Powel worked on ideas to turn the team around. When he noticed that attendance was down during weekday games because most people worked during the day, he changed the game forever. The Cincinnati Reds were the first team to introduce night games to major-league baseball.

Powel hired General Electric to design a new type of lighting system that would light the field as bright as the sun. GE's new bulbs were installed permanently on the newly named Crosley Field and then eventually added to other parks throughout the league.

It wasn't long before Powel extended the power of his radio station. Eventually, under special license from a newly created FCC, he was allowed to broadcast at 500,000 watts. This was ten times higher than his nearest competitor. The broadcast was so powerful that Powel could cover the United States in radio waves from his Cincinnati studio. From that day forward, his station was forever known as the "nation's station." The signal was so strong that it lit up light bulbs in houses located near the transmitter. This, along with complaints from other stations, eventually resulted in the Senate passing a bill that limited the broadcasting strength to 50,000 watts.

Radio wasn't Powel's only interest. By the late 1920s, Powel was a millionaire many times over. His restlessness had him starting and creating even more companies. Powel, along with Julius Fleischmann, the yeast and whisky king, started a plane manufacturing company and an airline. Their Mason Dixon Air Lines was a daily air service from Cincinnati to Detroit.

They had grand plans to fly throughout the South and even down to South America. For some reason, they changed their minds. Shortly after they incorporated, and just before the great stock-market crash of 1929, they sold their interests in the airline. Fleischmann took this opportunity and good fortune to sail around the world on his yacht. Crosley went back to selling radios. The airline they started went on as well. Through merger after merger, the airline survived, eventually changing its name to American Airlines.

For all of Powel's success in radios and consumer appliances, his first love was always automobiles. As a teenager, along with his brother, he built a motorized buckboard wagon that fascinated the town. By 1907, at age twenty-one, he had raised enough money to start a car company. The Marathon Six was the right car at the wrong time. Before he could ramp up production to more than the six cars, a downturn in the economy dried up sales and funding. By his twenty-second birthday, he had to shut the doors. A year later, he had recovered and began to invent again.

Powel's first successful invention of this new creative period was a tire liner. Early tires were very soft. They were prone to wear out quickly. It wasn't unusual to see a driver on the side of the road fixing a flat tire two or three times during a day's trip. Powell invented a unique tire liner that, when installed in a tire, could extend the life of the tire many times over. The success of the tire liner encouraged Powell to create other accessories for automobiles. Before long, he had a burgeoning mail-order business.

By 1939, the Crosley name was on everything from refrigerators and airplanes to phonographs, radios, and bikes. During the war years, the Crosley name was even on bombs for the military. But despite his success, Powel really wanted to build cars. In 1939, he started Crosley Motors. He set out to build a small inexpensive car. He bypassed the traditional dealers and sold his cars through his regular distribution channels.

Soon appliance and department stores were stocking the tiny Crosley car. It was small and light, which helped it achieve gas mileage between forty and fifty MPG. This was a major selling point during the gas-rationing days of WWII. Late in the forties, Crosley added a sports model. The Hotshot, as it was called, was the first American sports car. Despite some serious reliability problems, the car had some impressive success at auto races.

Unfortunately, even the new models couldn't save Crosley Motors. With wartime gas rationing over, the buying public was no longer interested in tiny, light, utilitarian cars, especially ones with reliability problems. Crosley Motors was finished. In 1952, Crosley Motors closed for good after producing over 75,000 cars in just ten years.

A lifetime of success couldn't ease the pain of Crosley having failed once again in the car manufacturing business. Crosley Motors was his last venture. He had sold his radio and broadcast interests after the war. The new owner failed to achieve the success of Powel Crosley and his brother. The Crosley Company stopped manufacturing in 1956. This brought an end to one of the most successful brands in history.

Crosley did keep one of his earlier holdings, the Cincinnati Reds baseball team. After his death in 1962, the Crosley Foundation sold the team, closing the final chapter on a remarkable career.

19 Who's Going to Be Responsible for This?: Robert Morris

It's funny how some incredibly famous and important people are forgotten by history while others who have made less of an impact are remembered or enshrined. Robert Morris is one of those significant figures who seems to have been lost in history. Morris is one of only two men who can claim to have signed not only the Declaration of Independence but also the Articles of Confederation and the final Constitution of the United States. But the story of Morris's contribution doesn't stop at these three documents.

At the start of the American Revolution, Robert Morris was one of the most respected and successful men in Philadelphia. His stellar reputation and his keen financial mind made him the ideal choice for superintendent of finance for what was then the newly formed United States of America.

As superintendent, Morris's role was to manage the finances of the country in its effort to support the ongoing war against Britain. With the treasury already $25 million in debt and the credit and credibility of the new nation in tatters, his job was not easy. Morris's first order of business was to create the Bank of North America. This was the first and only nationally chartered bank in the Americas. Morris lobbied hard and succeeded in persuading France to be the first depositor.

Using unprecedented dictatorial powers, Morris set about raising money for the bank. This money would subsequently be used to fund the war effort. In order to raise the funds to be used for Washington's army, Morris needed to co-sign notes as a personal guarantor. During the battle of Yorktown, Morris acted as quartermaster and personally bought or guaranteed the repayment of $1.4 million in notes. Within time, Morris committed the bulk of his fortune and credit to further the cause of the revolution by funding the war. Morris commented after the battle that the war had changed from a war of bullets to a war of money.

Morris's contribution as superintendent of finance to the creation of the United States economic system was invaluable. Morris's paper "On Public Credit" was the framework that Alexander Hamilton used to form the country's financial system. Morris was the first to use the two vertical bars that go through an "S" as the insignia now universally recognized as the dollar sign indicating the amounts for US currency.

But Morris didn't stop at just supplying money to the war effort. On one occasion, when supplies of bullets ran short, Morris organized a group of men to go from house to house and business to business to collect lead to be recycled into ammunition for the troops. Even the ballasts on his ships were stripped of lead to be donated to the war effort.

When the war ended, Morris's role had been seen as invaluable. While he was still a member of the Continental Congress, it was Robert Morris who nominated his friend General George Washington to be the first president of the United States.

George Washington was so impressed with Morris's work as the superintendent of finance, and his backing of the war effort, that he was Washington's first pick as secretary of the treasury.

History as we know it might be different if Morris had accepted Washington's appointment. Morris was still a wealthy man, but he had depleted a large part his personal cash and credit during the war years. Morris believed that he needed to get back to work to rebuild his fortune. He turned down Washington's appointment. Morris recommended that Washington select another friend of his, Alexander Hamilton. Hamilton accepted the appointment.

Morris's decision to go back to private enterprise was very rewarding … at first. Having lost over 150 of his trading ships during the war, Morris turned to land speculation to rebuild his fortune. His first transaction—3,750,000 acres of land that comprised a good chunk of western New York—was purchased from the state of Massachusetts for the sum of $333,333.33, after the previous borrowers defaulted on a million-dollar note. This purchase turned out to be very profitable. Morris leveraged this success into other land deals and eventually controlled over six million acres of land in the rural South and Washington DC.

Unfortunately for Morris, and for so many people before and after him, economic conditions are rarely predictable. By 1797, the young republic's economy, along with England's, collapsed. England's economy collapsed from the high costs associated with the exploding French revolutionary wars. The US economy collapsed from land speculation that had raised land prices far above sustainable levels. Investors and lending institutions did not want to loan money on overpriced real estate. This resulted in a freeze in the credit markets. As notes came due, the speculators couldn't obtain sufficient funds to meet the payments.

Having invested all his money in land and the US war effort, Morris didn't have enough hard currency to pay his debts to creditors when the notes came due.

Without additional credit to finance his land or the ability to sell the land, he was quickly facing the prospect of debtor's prison. Morris attempted to avoid his creditors by hiding out in his home. But his creditors pursued him right up to the gates and demanded that he come out and stand trial. Morris was arrested, convicted, and imprisoned for nonpayment of debts. He was sent to the Prune Street prison in Philadelphia in 1797.

Many of Morris' political adversaries used his financial failure to discredit him and seize power from the Federalists in Congress. It was Morris's friends in Congress, including two of his oldest friends, President George Washington and Alexander Hamilton, who came to his aid. They believed it was unfair that someone who had done so much for the birth of the nation should be behind bars. After all, Morris had signed his name to the Declaration of Independence, whereby, in effect, he had risked his life for his new country. He had put all his money and credit at the disposal of Washington's army. He was one of the main architects of America's financial system. After such sacrifice, it was manifestly unfair that he was destined to rot in jail. Unfortunately, there was nothing that could be done. Morris had to serve his prison term or pay back his debts. Seeing this as a great injustice, Morris's powerful friends began to lobby Congress for a solution. After much debate, Congress enacted a Bankruptcy Act. This act allowed debtors to avoid a debtor's prison and wipe out their debts if they liquidated their assets. The Bankruptcy Act of 1800 was instrumental in getting Morris released from debtor's prison. It was also instrumental in letting many others not pay their bills. As a result, after four short years, well after Morris was released from jail, Congress was forced to repeal the Bankruptcy Act.

It took almost a hundred years before Congress tackled this thorny subject again. Today, there is a bankruptcy law. But there is no longer a debtor's prison.

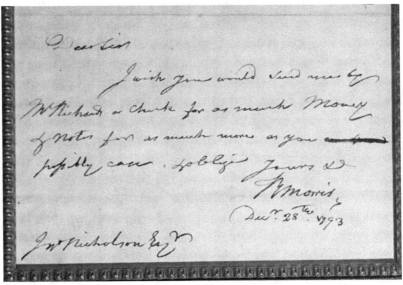

Handwritten document signed by Robert Morris. Morris writes
a friend to please send as much money and notes as he can.
Morris was always looking to raise cash for his investments in
real estate.

20 It's Electrifying!: Samuel Insull

When young Samuel Insull answered an ad in a London newspaper for a private secretary, he had no idea that the person who placed the ad was a representative in England for Thomas Edison. He didn't know that his skills as a clerk would catch the eye of the prolific inventor back in Menlo Park, New Jersey.

Insull's detailed reports were so complete, and his tenacious work ethic was so impressive, that the Wizard of Menlo Park encouraged young Samuel to emigrate to the United States to be his personal private secretary.

Thomas Edison relied heavily on Insull's talent and organizational skills. When Edison invented the light bulb and subsequently the Direct Current (DC) electrical system that powered it, it was up to Insull to help get the project off the ground. It was Insull, not Edison, who negotiated with the New York bankers to raise money for this ambitious project.

With businesses and homes wanting more of Edison's electric light, it soon became clear to Edison that more generating plants were needed. There were limitations to DC. It required that a dynamo be placed every four miles in order to assure a steady flow of strong electrical current. Edison needed to manufacture every part of the system he had designed. This included the dynamos, switches, and transformers that went into every new plant.

Insull's quick grasp of negotiating and organizational skills, and his knowledge of the issues, facts, and figures, quickly made him Edison's choice to head up the manufacturing division of the Edison Machine Works in upstate New York. Edison picked Insull to lead a group of Edison pioneers. They were charged with creating and building the parts needed to power the lights to be installed in New York City. It was in the Edison Machine Works building that the small Edison General Electric was operating.

By the late 1880s, a new competitor came onto the scene: Westinghouse. Westinghouse had teamed with Nicola Tesla, one of Edison's protégés. Together, they touted Alternating Current electricity as the wave of the future. AC provided great advantages over DC. The most important advantage was the ability to send electricity greater distances over power lines without a reduction in current.

AC could be sent out at very high voltages. At the point of use, it was simply stepped down to a lower voltage with small transformers. This was done to meet the lower power requirements necessary to run household lighting, appliances, and low-voltage industrial equipment. This use of higher voltages allowed AC to travel hundreds of miles past Edison's DC current, which had a two-and-a-half-mile restriction. Despite AC's advantages, Edison for his part was still holding on to DC as a safer alternative. The battle between Edison and Westinghouse increased, but it was soon clear that Edison was losing. With the backing of Edison's largest investor, the famous international banker J. P. Morgan, Edison was bought out of the company he had founded. Shortly after Edison's departure, Morgan arranged a merger between Edison General Electric and Thompson-Houston Electric.

Thompson-Houston Electric held the important patents for manufacturing dynamos. Even more important, Thompson-Houston held the patents for AC power generation. These patents helped the new company move into a more efficient AC generation.

It was Morgan who suggested that Edison be dropped from the name of the original company.

The companies were reorganized and combined under the shorter name General Electric. Insull, for his contribution, was made vice president of the new company. He was eventually offered the presidency, which he declined. Insull had bigger plans.

Months earlier, Insull had received a letter from the board of directors of Chicago Edison, a city-licensed power provider not owned by Edison or the new General Electric. The board was requesting recommendations from Insull for a new president to head their company. Insull recommended himself. He applied for the job, saying, "It is the best opportunity that I know of in the United States to develop the business of the production and distribution of electrical energy."

Chicago Edison Electric had a mere five thousand customers. The city of Chicago had a population of over one million. There were more than thirty small power companies fighting for a few thousand more customers. None of them were large enough to efficiently meet the needs of such a potentially huge customer base. Insull recognized that power generation was a declining-cost industry. That meant the more customers you have, the less you have to charge for your product however it is defined.

With a large enough power-generation base, an infinite number of customers could be enrolled without adding significant cost. This meant the only way to survive and profit was for one electric company to gain a monopoly. Once the monopoly was obtained, it would be self-perpetuating; no competitor could enter the business because it would have to charge significantly higher rates because of cost of equipment spread over a small customer base. Insull was successful in buying up most of the small competitors. He created a monopoly on power generation in Chicago. This monopoly of the power-generation capability allowed him to add customers quickly. The more customers he added reduced the cost per customer.

Insull's success with Chicago Edison attracted a powerful group of politically connected investors. They set up a company to compete for a new power-supply franchise that was being offered by the city of Chicago. Because of political connections, the new shell company, Commonwealth Electric and Power, was awarded the franchise. However, the investors were not interested in operating a power company in the city. They were really hoping to put pressure on Insull to force him to buy out their interest in Commonwealth at a large profit. Insull wasn't interested. He turned the tables on Commonwealth investors. He bought up all of the manufacturing inventory and capacity of the only two manufacturers of dynamos and transformers around: Westinghouse and General Electric.

Without the ability to build a plant and produce electricity, Commonwealth was not a threat to Chicago Electric. Insull bought Commonwealth from the investors for a mere $50,000. With it came the award of the Chicago franchise.

Insull merged the two companies. He combined the names into Commonwealth Edison and proceeded to build the largest power-generating station in the world. It was a big gamble. The market for electricity was still small. The cost of running such a big generating station was prohibitive if customers didn't come on quickly. A generating station large enough to power the city of Chicago is not something that can be turned off and on, or even slowed down. Unused electricity cannot be stored or used for later. With so much extra power coming from the station that couldn't be used, Commonwealth was losing money on every kilowatt sold. As in any declining-cost industry, especially power generation, a customer base must be built that will at least reach a break-even point.

Insull did everything he could think of to spur electricity usage. When he noticed much of his power went to waste at night, he lowered prices in the evening non-peak hours. He raised them during the day for businesses. He created the first electric-appliance financing plan to encourage consumers to step up their purchase of these labor-saving devices and increase their power consumption. Ever the visionary, he invested in and eventually controlled or owned many of the electrified railway systems in the city.

With electric usage steadily growing and cost per kilowatt used steadily coming down, Insull was able to showcase the company during the 1893 World's Columbian Exhibition in Chicago. The debut of George Washington Ferris's new amusement ride thrilled the crowd with its thirteen hundred light bulbs that illuminated the two-hundred-and-sixty-foot rotating structure. Lights burned bright at every corner of the exhibition. All were powered by Insull's dynamos.

At first, Insull was satisfied with serving only Chicago and the surrounding areas. But soon he came to recognize the potential of a national power grid using AC power. Insull believed such a grid would not only serve cities but also rural areas. To finance the expansion, Insull created a holding company. He sold nonvoting shares to the public. Most of the buyers were small individuals. Many were customers of Commonwealth Edison.

Insull used the money raised to expand his empire throughout the Midwest. He eventually reached South Dakota, then southeast to Florida and up into New England. In most of these states, Insull supplied the electricity that lit homes and powered the electrified transportation systems.

By 1912, Insull had control of so many electrified transportation systems that he formed a new holding company called Middle West Utilities Company. With the proceeds from the funds of the sale of stock to the public, Insull controlled or purchased outright over thirty companies in twenty states. Insull was creating the largest utility empire in the world, one which would top $3 billion in value by 1929.

Insull then acquired other types of businesses that he believed would increase the need for the power he generated. When the textile industry was collapsing in New England, Insull stepped in and purchased the failing mills in order to keep the employees working in the factories. These investments weren't that far-fetched.

The textile mills were next to waterfalls that were able to turn dynamos into the ability to generate cheap hydroelectric power. He sold this power not only to the mills but also to the workers who were employed by these mills. Insull could afford to lose money on the mills as long as he could generate cheap electricity from the waterfalls to sell back to the employees, residents, and businesses of New England.

By the mid 1920s, Insull controlled or owned outright electric, gas, and transportation companies in thirty-two states. His labyrinth of holding companies and trusts served over ten million people. They generated one-eighth of the electricity in the United States. His companies were earning over half a billion dollars a year in revenue. Insull's personal fortune was estimated to be in excess of $100 million. Insull had built the largest utility empire in US history.

Insull's vast holdings were tested during the 1929 stock-market crash, but his holdings held up well. Electric usage was still increasing. He was convinced the downturn would be short. Insull was so confident that he lent money and securities to friends and family to cover their personal margin calls so they would not to be swept away in the panic.

Although electric usage was on the rise, things weren't looking so good for Insull's transit system. The ridership on the railway system was drastically falling. In the first year, after the crash, the rail ridership dropped by thirteen million people. The second year, it dropped by thirty million more. At first, Insull was able to weather the downturn by using reserves that he had built up during better times.

When President Hoover declared in 1931 that the recession was over, Insull optimistically believed him. He opened the tap and poured money into numerous projects. He invested $8 million in a new Texas gas pipeline. He put $197 million into capital improvements to his power system. And he spent $500 million to bail out and revitalize Chicago's transit system. Insull also advanced $100 million to the almost bankrupt city of Chicago so the city could pay its teachers, firemen, and police force. Much of the money that he borrowed was personally guaranteed. To Insull's dismay, the economy never rebounded. All he could say was, "I was fooled, and so was the president."

It was soon apparent that Insull's empire, though large, had been built on a weak foundation. Insull had paid dearly for each of his acquisitions. He had borrowed heavily to complete them. To keep the companies solvent through these difficult times, Insull was able to arrange for a $10 million loan from his biggest suppliers, GE and Westinghouse. As the economic downturn continued, he found himself looking for extensions on his loans. He had to go hat in hand to a source he came to despise, the New York bankers on Wall Street.

The president of GE, Owen Young, who was head of the New York Federal Reserve, arranged a meeting. He agreed to mediate between Insull and the banks. The meeting had barely started when J. P. Morgan arrived. He asked Insull to step outside while he spoke with the others. Several minutes later, when Young emerged from the room, he informed Insull there would be no extension. Insull left the building in tears. One by one, each of Insull's companies collapsed into receivership. He couldn't redeem or refinance his debt. During the ensuing stock-market collapse, Insull's companies lost $750 million in value. Insull had hundreds of millions in assets but only $27 million in equity.

Insull stayed on the board of each of his companies to help reorganize. Slowly, one by one, he resigned his positions when it became apparent that the public was looking for a scapegoat. Six hundred thousand shareholders, mostly lower- and middle-class investors who Insull had pursued to invest in the companies, lost everything.

His investors, the city of Chicago, and even the federal government were all after him. He endured hounding newsmen, photographers, and even death threats. When it became clear that the federal government was going to indict him for fraud, Samuel Insull left the country. First he went to Paris, and eventually he settled in Greece. For months, authorities chased Insull and tried to get him back to the United States to stand trial. Greece did not have an extradition treaty with the United States, so the authorities there refused to send Insull back. But when it became clear that Greece would not renew his visa, Insull took a steamer provided by an English friend and went to Romania. He was not allowed to land in Romania. He continued to Turkey, only to have his steamer stopped by Turkish authorities who placed him in an Istanbul jail to await extradition back to the United States.

After eighteen months out of the country, Samuel Insull was headed back home to stand trial for mail fraud, bankruptcy fraud, embezzlement, and antitrust charges. After a lengthy trial, where he was crucified and vilified in the press, a bankrupt Samuel Insull was acquitted on all charges.

Immediately after the trial, Insull and his wife, Gladys, left Chicago. They settled in Paris, where they lived in a small apartment. Gladys and Samuel vowed never to return to the Windy City. Insull, the once mighty millionaire and utility baron, lived on a $21,000 pension he received from one of the surviving entities he had created. Four years after the trial, Insull walked down a flight of stairs in a Paris subway station and collapsed from a heart attack. As he lay there dying on the platform floor, his wallet was stolen. With only a few francs in his pocket, this man who helped to found General Electric and had once been on top of the most successful utility empires in the world—not to mention the unifier of the Chicago electrified train system—lay dead on the floor of a railway station. He was an unidentified, apparently homeless man.

By the 1940s, with the Depression over, Insull's securities rebounded. The people who held on to their investments in all of Insull's companies eventually recovered their principle and made a tidy profit. The bankers, led by J. P. Morgan, who refused to extend a mere $20 million loan to Insull were also holding securities worth millions of dollars.

21 You Reap What You Sew: Isaac Merritt Singer

The saying goes, "Success has many fathers, and failure is an orphan." So it is with the development of the sewing machine, one of those inventions that had many "fathers."

A sewing machine was first proposed in 1790 by an Englishman, Thomas Saint. Over the next fifty years, many inventors tinkered with and added to the basic premise and efficiency of the machine. It wasn't until 1846, when inventor Elias Howe created the lockstitch and moving shuttle, that a practical (but still unreliable) sewing machine showed up in the marketplace.

After lining up investors in England and returning home, Howe was angered to learn that dozens of companies were manufacturing sewing machines. Each and every one of them was infringing on his patents. One of those companies was owned by Isaac Merritt Singer.

Singer never set out to become a manufacturer or even a businessman. Singer's real love was acting. Not unlike the actors of today, many of whom have to wait tables for a steady paycheck until they get their lucky break; Singer had to leave the stage from time to time to earn a living. During the lean times, he took jobs in workshops or hired out as manual labor. Singer was working with his brother on a tunnel-digging project in Chicago when he got the idea for his first invention. It was a drill bit that would go through rock. This new drill bit was his ticket back to the stage.

Singer was not interested in operating a company to manufacture drill bits. He sold the patent he had obtained for his invention for $2,000. This was more money than he had ever seen in his lifetime. It was enough to get him back onstage.

With his newfound wealth, Singer started his own acting troupe. It was called the Merritt Players. He set out on the road with his new wife by his side. Both of them were actors.

It took five years, but eventually the money ran out. Singer was back looking for work and tried his hand again at inventing. It wasn't long before he received a letter from Orson Phelps, the proprietor of a machine shop in Massachusetts. Phelps invited Singer to set up one of Phelps's new inventions, a block-carving machine. It was in that Boston shop that Singer stumbled upon the invention that would change his life and modernize the textile industry.

Orson Phelps's shop was in the business of manufacturing sewing machines. The truth was that the workers were spending more time repairing the machines than making new machines to sell. Phelps's frustration with the unreliable machines was what caused him to seek out Singer's advice to find a solution.

Knowing Singer was a handy workman and inventor, Phelps brought him into the back room and asked if he could fix the broken machines. Singer quickly determined that the design was faulty. That's what was causing the problems. Phelps was skeptical that Singer's quick assessment could solve the problems. He told Singer, "If you can make a really practical sewing machine, you will make more money in a year than you can in fifty with that carving affair."

That statement was more than enough motivation for Singer. He immediately went to work on the sewing-machine problem. He worked day and night for eleven days until he came up with a new, practical, and reliable design. His design replaced the curved needle and circular shuttle that had been causing the problems.

He replaced it with a straight needle and forward-moving shuttle that were much simpler to manufacture and operate. These basic changes are still reflected in the way sewing machines are made today.

To create the first prototype for his new sewing machine, Singer raised forty dollars from an associate named Zieber. He also had help from Phelps. Singer, Phelps, and Zieber were now partners.

Singer received a patent for his designs in 1851. He was soon manufacturing and marketing a very reliable sewing machine at a cost of $125. Sales continued to grow. Singer didn't see that his new partners were of much value to him. He worked ruthlessly, first to get rid of Phelps. Then, when Zieber grew deathly ill, he convinced his partner to sell his stock to him. Singer promised that he would take care of Zieber's family after the man's death.

With the company's stock in hand, Singer hired the best doctor he could find to nurse Zieber back to health. He didn't want to be burdened with caring for the man's family.

As the company grew, Singer found himself, along with other manufacturers, tied up in a patent suit with Howe. Legal costs were crushing Singer. He refused to pay Howe a red cent as a royalty.

Singer, with his back against the wall, turned to Edward Clark, a prominent lawyer and ex-Sunday school teacher. Clark's wife wasn't fond of Singer. Singer had a bad reputation. She urged Clark not to go into business with "that nasty brute."

Clark saw the potential of the sewing machine. He agreed to take a 50 percent stake in Singer's company in lieu of payment to fight Howe in court. It took years, but Howe finally won the case against Singer. Singer was required to pay a huge sum of money to Howe, but by that time, Singer had more than enough money.

Still, there were many conflicting patents issued in the development of the sewing machine. With the cost of legal proceedings crippling the companies, the group of patent holders finally agreed to combine their patents, and this included Howe's.

They set out to manufacture their products under the "Sewing Machine Combination." The I. M. Singer Company was one of the first to sign on in the patent pool.

Singer was not a well-educated man. For the most part, he was illiterate. He let Clark, who had truly brilliant management skills, run the company. Singer's job was to market and promote the sewing machine. It was because of Clark's talents that the company grew into one of the first truly multinational corporations of the time.

As time went by, the conservative and proper Clark became very concerned about Singer's reputation as a ladies' man. He convinced Singer that it would be best for the company if Singer were to step down from the day-to-day management. Singer accepted this suggestion as long as Clark did not succeed him as president of the company until after Singer's death.

To fill the president's role when Singer stepped down, they agreed to make an office boy by the name of Inslee Hopper the president. They paid him the princely sum of twenty dollars a week. Eventually, they raised Hopper's salary to thirty dollars a week, and then to $6,000 a year. Even in those days, this was a nominal amount for the job of running a multinational enterprise.

Even though Hopper was president, Clark was still firmly in control. Singer went off to enjoy the life of a millionaire. He built elaborate coaches and mansions, and he chased women. Clark continued the daily grind of running the Singer Sewing Machine Company. He also managed to help Singer invest his vast wealth from the Singer Sewing Machine Company.

Part of the money was invested in real estate. One of their earliest investments was the Dakota apartment building in Manhattan. You might remember it as the home of John Lennon and Yoko Ono—and the place where John Lennon was killed.

As it turns out, Singer's personal life was much more interesting than his business one. Singer was not only illiterate, but also a wanton philander. Singer had a habit of starting families with women and fathering children while neglecting to divorce his former wives. His first wife, who had accepted the arrangement, was incensed when she saw Singer in an opulent yellow carriage, drawn by twelve black horses, driving down Fifth Avenue in New York with his second wife.

As time went by, she had enough. She went to the police and filed a charge of bigamy. Singer was arrested but was quickly released on bail.

While free on bond, Singer decided it was time to leave the country. He skipped bail. He and his second family left by ship for London. Interestingly enough, a third family that his first wife didn't know about lived under the surname of Merritt in lower Manhattan.

This was by no means the end of Singer's affairs. During a trip to Paris, he met and married Isabella Eugenie Boyer. She had left her husband because she was pregnant with Isaacs's child. Isabella Eugenie Boyer was considered one of the most beautiful women in Europe. She is purportedly the model for the Statue of Liberty. Like his other legal and common-law wives, she didn't take the Singer name. She went by Isabella Somerville.

Singer and Isabella left Paris for England shortly after the wedding. Singer built a 115-room mansion so he could live with and entertain his many children, grandchildren, multiple wives, and girlfriends. At the time of his death in 1875, Singer had twenty-eight surviving children and scores of grandchildren. He also left behind as many as twenty-two legal or common-law wives and girlfriends. They all claimed part of his estate. After years of litigation, it was Isabella who was declared his sole legal wife. She was entitled to her share of his $14 million estate.

The story of Isaac Singer's legacy doesn't stop there. Singer's heirs melted into European society. Some of them even married royalty. But it was granddaughter Daisy Singer Alexander who made news in the United States.

The story goes that in 1937, Daisy wrote a brief will shortly before her death. She placed the will in a bottle and threw it into the Thames River in London. The bottle floated for twelve years. It was untouched until in 1949, when it completed a 10,000 mile journey and washed up on a beach in San Francisco. An unemployed restaurant worker and beachcomber named Jack Wurm found the bottle. He noticed that it had a cargo. Much to his astonishment, when Jack opened the bottle, he found the will of Daisy Singer Alexander. The will simply stated, "To avoid any confusion, I leave my entire estate to the lucky person who finds this bottle and to my attorney, Barry Cohen, share and share alike.—Daisy Alexander, June 20, 1937." The proceeds to be split amounted to $6 million, plus stock income of $80,000 a year in dividends.

Jack Wurm made the news with this find. He quickly contacted solicitor Cohen in London. He informed Cohen about the bottle and asked how he might claim his good fortune. Cohen was suspicious, but he did have to admit to the press that no other will had ever surfaced. Members of Daisy's household staff and even close friends believed that this unlikely document was indeed her will. Some even claimed to have heard Daisy talk about putting her will in a bottle and throwing it in the Thames.

It is doubtful that Mr. Wurm or Mr. Cohen ever shared Daisy's fortune. As of 1954, Jack Wurm was still working in a downtown San Francisco restaurant. He had to admit to the newspapers that he was still waiting for his share of the Singer fortune. Daisy, like her grandfather, left enough intrigue upon her death to keep an army of lawyers busy for a lifetime.

22 Two Tons of What?: Thomas Adams

Some products are born of necessity. Some come from genius and still others from dumb luck. Thomas Adams's success came from a chance meeting—actually, two chance meetings.

One of Thomas Adams's early endeavors was photography. Photography was a new field in the 1860s. It was popularized in the United States by Mathew Brady, who hired numerous men to photograph the events of the Civil War. History didn't record whether Adams was one of Brady's photographers. What we do know is that Adams quit photography sometime in the late 1860s to pursue other interests and to make a better living.

Adams's true passion was inventing. He was always looking for a good idea or a new challenge. His biggest challenge—and the one that propelled him to riches—came about at his home in Staten Island, New York. The visitor, who was boarding with him at the time, was none was none other than Antonio de Padua Maria Severino López de Santa Anna y Pérez de Lebrón. To most Americans, this Mexican gentleman is known simply as General Antonio Santa Anna. It was General Santa Anna who was the leader of the Mexican Army that defeated a small band of defenders at the Alamo in Texas in 1835.

Santa Anna's triumph at the Alamo was short-lived. His next battle, against Sam Houston at the battle of San Jacinto, resulted in a crushing defeat, which sent his army back to Mexico and sent General Santa Anna into exile. This is just one of the many times he was forced to leave Mexico in disgrace. By 1855, the general had worn out his welcome and was driven out of Mexico. Cuba was his first stop. He eventually landed in the United States on the doorstep of Thomas Adams in Staten Island, New York, in 1870.

When he met Adams, Santa Anna had been exiled from Mexico for over fifteen years. But he never gave up wanting to return to Mexico to regain his place as president. To do so, he certainly needed an army. To that end, he solicited the help of his new aide, Thomas Adams. Santa Anna was not able to raise money for his army. He had to earn what he needed.

During a late-night chat in Adams's living room, the general became intrigued with Adams's knowledge of chemistry and his interest in inventing. The general made Adams a proposition. Santa Anna wanted access to sap from the sapodilla tree. The general explained to Adams that the sap, which was known as *chicle* in Mexico, might be used to lower the cost of rubber production or maybe even replace rubber altogether. The first person to find a rubber replacement would definitely make a fortune. Santa Anna was sure that with Adams's help, he would make his fortune by supplying chicle from the sapodilla tree to be used as a replacement or extender for rubber. With his new riches, Santa Anna would have no trouble raising an army for his powerful, triumphant return to Mexico.

Intrigued, Adams agreed to buy a shipment of chicle from the general to start experimenting. Santa Anna arranged for his friends in Mexico to deliver what must have been two tons of chicle to a warehouse in New York for Adams to begin the experiments.

Adams, along with his son, set out to transform the sap into practical and useful products. They used a vulcanizing process that was similar to the one developed to create tires by Charles Goodyear. Unfortunately for Adams and Santa Anna, they could not find a practical use for the sticky substance. Adams worked and experimented for over a year to try to make tires, rain boots, toys, and even masks. He just couldn't find a replacement for rubber or any other practical use for the stuff.

Adams was just about ready to throw the remaining stock of chicle into the East River when he happened on a new possibility. While he was at local drugstore, a young girl entered. She bought what appeared to be a small wrapped piece of gum. The item cost a penny. When Adams asked the clerk what the gum was made of, the clerk said that it was a paraffin wax called White Mountain. Adams immediately thought, "What about gum out of chicle?" Santa Anna had been chewing the gum while he was a guest at Adams's house. Even Adams himself chewed the gum with his son while they experimented with the rubber products. If Adams was right about chicle being made into chewing gum, he could salvage the remaining stock at the Front Street warehouse.

Adams left the store excited. He explained the idea to his son, Tom Jr., who thought it just might work. Adams and his son cut the remaining chicle into pieces that were the same size as the wax pieces sold in the drugstore for a penny. Adams wrapped the gum in colored tissue paper. He created dollar boxes that he called Adams's New York No. 1 Snapping and Stretching Gum. It was pure chicle and was not flavored. Tom Jr., who had a job as a salesman in the wholesale tailor and trimming trade, agreed to take boxes with him on his travels. He tried to sell the gum to drugstores in between his regular sales calls.

When Tom Jr. returned, he told his father that he couldn't sell a single box. He did, however, promise to try again on his next trip out west. On his next trip, Tom Jr. took a different approach. He offered the drugstore owner a box of Adams' New York Gum on consignment. All the drugstore owner had to do was display the box prominently on the store's counter. This approach worked. Within days, he placed the entire inventory of twenty-five boxes. When he returned home, Tom Jr. found that his father had received reorders for three hundred boxes of Adams' New York No. 1. He was struggling to keep up with the demand.

Tom Jr. was so encouraged with the initial orders that he quit his job as a wholesale salesman in the tailor and trimming industry and began to sell gum for the newly formed Adams Chewing Gum Company. Together they rented a small building in New Jersey. Thirty girls were hired to cut and wrap chicle into penny sticks. Soon, New York No. 2, a larger pack of gum, was introduced. The orders rolled in so quickly that the small army of girls couldn't keep up. Tom Adams Sr. set out to invent a machine to keep up with demand. He worked day and night. Finally, in 1871, he patented the first machine to make penny gum.

By 1875, the Adams's had a thriving business, but competition was nipping at their heels. To stay ahead of the competition, they introduced the first flavored chewing gum. They named the first licorice flavor "Black Jack." It was the first gum offered in flat sticks. Black Jack Gum, along with the Adams Company's other new flavor, Tutti Fruiti, went on to be the first product of any kind sold in a vending machine in America.

Santa Anna never did profit from the sale of chicle. He did, however, have a chance to return to his native Mexico in 1874 under an amnesty program. The general died two years later in 1876, penniless and heartbroken. He never knew that he was responsible for one of the single most popular confections in history.

23 Gentleman, Get Out of My Company!: William Durant

The company started by William Durant is an international household name, but history has all but forgotten the name of its founder.

Before Henry Ford, there was William (Willie) Capo Durant. Willie was born into a prominent Michigan family in the 1800s. He did not grow to be a very large person. In fact, he was quite small. But being small in stature did not keep him from developing a larger-than-life persona.

As a teen, while working in his uncle's lumberyard, Willie met Josiah Dort. Dort was a great craftsman who had a small woodworking shop that produced carriages. Durant took a keen interest in the business and soon joined with Dort to start the Coldwater Road Cart Company.

Willie had grand plans to increase the size of this new company. He knew that the quickest method to meet this objective was through acquisitions. So, shortly after he partnered with Dort, Willie began buying up competitors. He had a keen interest in one competitor in particular: a carriage maker in Indiana had come up with a design for putting leaf springs under the seat of buckboard wagons. When Willie test-rode a carriage manufactured by this competitor, it was like riding on a cloud. Willie was convinced that if anyone rode in the competitors invention, no one would buy his wagons.

Willie raced home and arranged a loan at the local bank to buy up the patents. From that day forward, all of the carriages of the Coldwater Road Cart Company, re-christened the Durant-Dort Carriage Company, had the newly patented spring seats. By 1890, the Durant-Dort Carriage Company was the largest manufacturer of carriages in the country.

Durant was a visionary with an uncanny ability to predict the future direction of business. When he saw the first horseless-carriage motor car, he knew it was only a matter of time before the largest carriage maker, Durant-Dort Carriage Company, would go out of business. So when investors with Buick Motor Cars came calling and asked Durant to join them as the general manager of their motor-car company, he seized the moment. In 1904, the Durant-Dort Carriage Company started building Buicks.

Durant was not interested in just building motor cars. He wanted to build many motor cars. During the early part of the 1900's, there were several hundred shops across the country building motor cars. Durant's plan was to buy out the competitors the same way he did in the carriage industry and merge them into one company.

Durant systematically approached each of the small competitors, and with his energy and consummate charm, he managed to get company after company to join him in his new venture. First Oldsmobile, then Oakland (later re-named Pontiac), then Cadillac, and the list goes on. In one year, he made over two hundred acquisitions. To make sure he had a steady flow of parts, Willie bought up parts suppliers as well. Dayton Engineering Laboratory Company (DELCO), Champion Spark Plugs, and the Hyatt Roller Bearing Company were just a few of the companies that were purchased. It was with the acquisition of Hyatt that he also acquired a future management genius named Alfred P. Sloan.

Durant had some of the greatest engineers of the time working for him in his little company: Walter Chrysler, Henry Leland (Cadillac), and Charles Kettering. It was Kettering who figured out how to install working lights on automobiles, and he also invented the first electric starter. Leland was the first to develop interchangeable parts. These two were "the best of the best," and they worked for Durant.

In 1910, Durant's energy and unrelenting deal making finally tripped him up. An economic downturn caused him to be overextended, which frightened his bankers. Thus, the unexpected occurred. The banks that had provided most of the capital Durant needed to grow his company walked in, took control, and fired him on the spot.

The downturn of 1910 quickly ended, but the bankers were still firmly in control. The banks ran the company to maximize profits. Slowly, they drained the company of money, energy, and talent. To the dismay of the stockholders, the stock began a steady decline.

Durant watched closely. He quickly set about starting a new car company. By this time, Henry Ford had come on the scene and was showing the world his new Model T. Durant decided to build a car to compete with the Model T and the Buick. His car wasn't going to be as bare-bones as the Model T or as expensive as the Buick. To accomplish his goal, he teamed up with a burly Swiss race-car driver named Louis Chevrolet. Durant thought Chevrolet was a great name for a car. Louis' racing experience would surely help in design and sales.

Almost from the beginning, the rough-edged Chevrolet and the sophisticated William C. Durant were at odds. But in spite of their turbulent relationship, they managed to manufacture a mid-priced car, and Durant proceeded to sell stock in the Chevrolet Company.

It wasn't long before Chevrolet cars were rolling off the assembly line. The public wanted whatever Durant was selling. They wanted the cars, and they wanted the stock. The stockholders in his previous company were not as happy. They watched helplessly as the value of their stock declined after Durant left. The bankers had managed to starve the company of cash by paying themselves handsomely.

Durant seized on the stockholders' dissatisfaction to get even. He offered holders of stock in his old company a swap proposition. He gave the old company's shareholders ten shares of his new company's stock in exchange for each share of stock they tendered to Willie. With Chevrolet stock skyrocketing and the other company's stock faltering, it was an "offer they couldn't refuse."

By 1916, Durant had accumulated enough shares in the old company to make his move. At the annual meeting, Durant walked casually into the boardroom and announced that he now had control of General Motors (the name given to the old company because of its conglomeration of different car builders). A flustered group of bankers couldn't believe what they heard. It was true. He sent the bankers packing, and Chevrolet became a new brand for General Motors.

Durant continued on his previous path. He never let up on making deals and acquiring car companies. He didn't learn his lesson, either. By 1920, he was overextended again. This time, there was no saving the company. Durant had used all of his money and credit to prop up GM during yet another economic downturn.

J. P. Morgan, who represented the DuPont family in the purchase of large blocks of stocks over the years, had had enough of Durant's freewheeling ways. In a late-night meeting, J. P. arranged a bailout of Durant and his company. Durant left the room penniless. He drove home and broke down and cried in his wife's arms. They had lost everything.

From then on, General Motors was firmly under the control of the DuPont family. Irene DuPont came out of retirement to run the company. A short time later, Alfred P. Sloan took the helm to grow the company into an international powerhouse.

Along the way, Sloan created new management techniques that are still being taught and studied in universities and corporate halls throughout the world.

Durant tried again, but failed, to start a car company. The industry had moved on past his talents. Now broke and in his later years, he was seen trying his hand at running a bowling alley in Detroit. His life had become less than the glamorous one he had known.

There is no happy ending to this story. Durant, the man who had created one of the largest industrial enterprises in the world and was once one of the richest and most powerful men in America, ended up living on handouts from friends—many of whom he had made millionaires.

DURANT MOTORS, INC.

FISK BUILDING
250 WEST FIFTY-SEVENTH STREET
NEW YORK

OFFICE OF THE PRESIDENT

March 13, 1925.

Mr. C. D. Willson,
El Mirasol,
Santa Barbara, Cal.

My dear Mr. Willson:-

         This will introduce my best friend,
Mr. John T. Smith, who at my suggestion is
stopping at Santa Barbara for a few moments
so that he may get a glimpse of the most
unique "resting place" in California and meet
(if I am any judge) a 100% manager and "comfort
caterer".

         Show him, if you will, the type
bungalow that we so thoroughly enjoyed, in the
hope that we may have the Smiths with us next
year.

         I regret to say that my plans since
writing you have been changed and that my trip
to California will be postponed until later in
the season.

Cordially yours,

Document signed by William Durant on Durant Motors letterhead. Durant started Durant Motors after he lost control of General Motors in 1920 to the DuPont family. Unfortunately he was not able to duplicate the success he had with Chevrolet and left the car business for good in 1931

24 Nickel and Dimed: Frank W. Woolworth

The name Woolworth is a corporate icon that is almost forgotten in history, unless you are over forty years old. Even so, it is still just a faint image of a simple dime store that seemed to lose its way.

F. W. Woolworth Co., with its distinctive red and gold storefront, closed its last US store in 1997. For over one hundred years, Woolworth's retail empire was a fixture in almost every city in the nation. Its name recognition was as high as, if not higher than, Coke, Nike, McDonalds, and Starbucks.

The story of Frank Woolworth and the Woolworth empire began in a small hardware store in Watertown, New York. Frank was an eager stock clerk. He had a talent for creating merchandise displays. It didn't hurt that he was willing to work for free just so he could learn the business. Today it is very common to display merchandise in an attractive way to entice a customer. In Woolworth's day, it was very unusual. When customers wanted something, the store clerk would simply go behind the counter to get it. With that method, most merchandise didn't move very quickly.

In order to get rid of excess stock, the store owner, Frank's employer filled a table with interesting items and priced them at five cents. Within a day, the table would be empty and the store owner delighted. This went on for several weeks until the fad wore off.

Nevertheless, Frank was hooked on retailing. He was especially hooked on five-cent retailing. Frank convinced his boss to sell him $300 worth of merchandise on credit. He was going to sell everything for five cents apiece and make a handsome profit.

With a suitcase full of his wares, Frank boarded a train to Utica, New York, to open his first store. With his limited funds, he rented a vacant shop on a side street. Frank papered the windows, to hide what he was doing from prying eyes, while he set up the merchandise inside. On opening day, he did well. But on the days that followed the grand opening, his sales fell off until they were barely a trickle. Utica wasn't very impressed with young Frank's method of selling. After little more than a year, Frank had to admit that his first store was a dismal failure.

With the remaining goods intact, Frank boarded a train back to Watertown. He got his job back at the old hardware store. But like every other entrepreneur before and after him, he had the bug. It was only a few months later that he decided to try again.

With suitcase in hand, he boarded the train for the second time. This time he headed to Lancaster, Pennsylvania. He rented a shop on the town's main street. Frank busied himself setting up the store. He printed flyers and placed ads to announce a special kind of new store. Even the signs on the windows announced that something exciting was coming.

Frank spent several days arranging the tables and decorating the windows. He was certain that the idea of the customer touching and selecting the merchandise at a cost of just five cents a piece was going to be a hit this time.

When opening day came, there was a line at the door. By the end of the day, young Frank had sold $121 worth of the five-cent items. The store was definitely going to be a success. Frank had found a formula that worked. He offered good products at value prices with a location on the main street in the heart of town. Sound familiar? Where do you think Wal-Mart got the idea?

It wasn't long before Frank opened more stores. To staff the new stores, he recruited his relatives and a few well-chosen partners. Everyone seemed to be clamoring for Frank's wares. There was such demand that, try as he might; he just couldn't hold prices to a nickel. In order to keep sales rising and offer a larger selection to his patrons, Frank added a ten-cent table. It wasn't long before F. W. Woolworth's, also known as the five and dime, was everywhere.

When Frank's store count reached 586, he believed the time was right to go public and sell stock. He liked to boast later in life that he created over a hundred millionaires that day.

In 1911, with his success secure and an enterprise spanning the globe, he decided to build a world headquarters. It was not just any building but the tallest building in the world. At a cost of $13.5 million, all paid in cash, he completed the Woolworth building in Manhattan. It remained the tallest building in the world until the opening of the Chrysler building more than twenty years later.

Not everything was perfect for Frank. His daughter, who married Frank Hutton, brother of E. F. Hutton, the senior partner in the famous stock brokerage company, had a bipolar illness. Pushed over the edge by her husband's overt affairs, she committed suicide. It was only a year later that Frank himself died of a tooth infection that could have been prevented had he not had a fear of dentists.

Frank's estate went to his family. The large share that was to go to his deceased daughter, Edna, was passed on to her daughter, Barbara. They say money doesn't buy happiness. Well, Barbara was the poster child for that saying.

Barbara was ignored by her father. She was bounced around to relatives, governesses, and boarding schools. On her eighteenth birthday, while the rest of the world was standing in breadlines, Barbara had a million-dollar coming out ball. The guest list included Vanderbilt's, Rockefellers, and Astor's. On Barbara's twenty-first birthday, the "poor little rich girl," as the tabloids called her, inherited $50 million (the equivalent of $1 billion today). That was at the height of the Depression.

Barbara spent her money wildly. She lived the life of a socialite jet-setter who had every luxury. She bought her way out of seven failed and abusive marriages. She died with just over $4,000 in the bank. She was famously quoted as saying, "I have never seen a Brinks Truck follow a hearse."

So what is left of Frank's legacy? Having spent more than a hundred years operating as Woolworth's, the company expanded into other businesses. One of its many acquisitions was a shoe store chain called Kinney Shoes. You might still shop at Kinney Shoes and not even know it. While you will no longer find a Woolworth five and dime in every town across America, Kinney Shoes, now under the new name of Foot Locker, is in every major mall across the globe. Now you know.

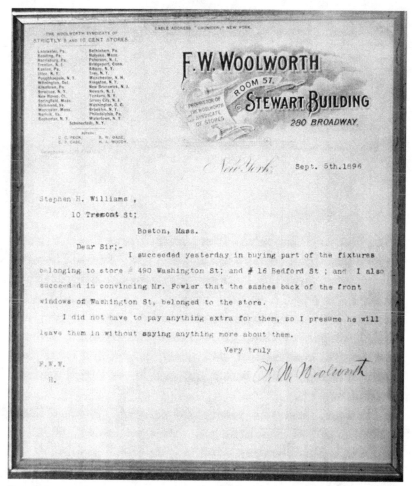

Document signed by Frank Woolworth on ornate company letterhead. Woolworth at the time was in headquartered in the Stewart building built by A.T.Stewart. The building was once the A.T. Stewart Dry Goods store. A.T. Stewarts Dry Goods was once the largest and most famous department store in America.

25 Out in the Cold: Armand Hammer

It has been said that behind every great fortune there's a crime. Those words speak volumes in the life of Dr. Armand Hammer. But Hammer wasn't just your everyday gangster, drug dealer, or swindler. He was the ultimate capitalist and power broker. He lived the life of a true capitalist. Surprising as it may seem, and with all the investigation into charges of bribery and espionage, he was never convicted or charged with anything other than a misdemeanor, which was attributed to an illegal political contribution.

Hammer, during his ninety-two years of life, was a friend or advisor to five presidents and six Soviet leaders, including Vladimir Lenin. Hammer was the king of self-promotion. He was so obsessed with power that he went to any means, and any cost, to achieve it. Once, when he was asked if he wanted to be president of the United States, he responded with, "Why? I make presidents." That was the arrogance and power that Hammer had.

Armand Hammer was born to Julius and Rose Hammer. He was not named for the famous Arm and Hammer baking soda, as some have suspected. His father named him after the arm and hammer that symbolized the American Socialist movement.

Armand's father, Julius, had a successful medical practice and also owned five drugstores in the Bronx, New York. Julius was a dedicated Socialist. As such, he was a founding member of the American Communist Party, which came to support the Russian Revolution. Whatever money Julius made in his business in the early 1900s went to support efforts to overthrow the czar. He even met Lenin himself and offered money and services to the Russian cause.

Armand, his older son, didn't care much for politics. He didn't share his father's passionate views on socialism. Armand did want to follow his father into medicine and become a doctor. But a strange turn of events changed everything and put Armand at the forefront of the Soviet cause.

During the Spanish flu epidemic of 1918, Julius was asked by a Russian dignitary to perform an abortion on the dignitary's daughter. The morning after he completed the procedure, he received a knock on the door. He was informed that his patient had died from complications. Julius was arrested and charged with manslaughter. Even though abortions were illegal at the time, doctors were not usually charged with a crime if it could be argued that the procedure was done to save the life of the mother. In this case, however—and probably because of Julius's political leanings—the judge gave Julius the maximum sentence. He was sentenced to twelve years of hard labor in Sing Sing Prison in upstate New York.

Later, one of Armand's mistresses claimed that Armand admitted to her that it was he who had performed the botched abortion that caused the death of the Russian girl, not his father.

Even from prison, Julius sent instructions through his son Armand to pay money to supply shipments to further support the Russian cause. While Julius was in prison, it was up to Armand and his brother, Victor, to run the family drug business. When Armand took over the business, he found that his father was deep in debt. This was primarily due to his support for the American

Socialist Party and the payments made to Russian operatives. There was also a great deal of money owed to Julius's company by the new Soviet regime that he had helped create.

Armand decided that in order to save the business, he had to go to Russia to collect the money due to the firm. He may have also delivered messages to the Soviet government. In any case, traveling to Russia was forbidden. Getting a passport that would allow travel to Russia was nearly impossible.

Armand had a plan. On his passport application, he claimed he was going to Europe for humanitarian purposes. He was going to help with the typhoid epidemic by delivering needed medical supplies. He also said that he was going to collect $150,000 owed to him by the Russian government. That was patently false.

The new head of the FBI, J. Edgar Hoover, knew it was not true. But Armand was allowed to travel anyway. Hoover believed that if he let Hammer go, the FBI would get more information on the Socialist movement than if they forbade him to travel.

When he arrived in St. Petersburg, Armand, through his father's contacts, met with Lenin himself. Lenin explained that Russia needed American technology and American investments if Russia's economy was to succeed. He believed that Armand was the man who could lead American businesses to Russia's door. He offered Armand the first concession for trade with the new government. It was Lenin's hope that other American business leaders would see Hammer's success in Russia and would want to participate in trade with this new and powerful nation. The meeting with Lenin changed Armand's path. He became Dr. Armand Hammer, the industrialist.

There was also a clandestine side to Armand's meeting with Lenin. Lenin not only needed American investments in the emerging Soviet Union, but he also needed hard currency as a way to pay the operatives and subversives in America. It was up to Armand to stand in for his father and launder Russian money in order to pay Russian operatives. Armand didn't much care for

Socialism or the Russian revolution. But he did care about money and power.

Armand's dealings with the Communist government were getting so big that even though Julius was serving a twelve-year sentence for manslaughter, he was able to get a compassionate release in order to help his son manage the family business. Upon his release from prison, Julius sailed to Russia. He was united with his wife, Rose, and his sons, who were all living a life of luxury in Moscow.

The Hammers lived in a thirty-five-room mansion in central Moscow. They entertained the many dignitaries who visited Russia looking for investment opportunities. The Hammers were in the perfect place to observe history as it was being made. Armand made many contacts during those days, many of which served him in his business dealings for the rest of his life. He also married a Russian cabaret singer who gave him a child.

After Lenin died and Stalin came into power, things started to change in Russia. Things also changed for the Hammers. Concessions that the Hammers had been given as payment for services were nationalized and taken away. But by no means were the Russians and the Hammers done doing business together. The Russians still needed hard cash from the West. Together, they had a plan.

One of the principle assets that the Soviets had was art that could be turned into cash—and lots of it. Much of the art had been confiscated from shops, factories, and the houses of aristocrats. The Russians and the Hammers devised a plan to sell some of the art pieces in the West.

Act Two for Armand was as an art dealer for the Russians. He arranged for Russian treasures to be shipped to America and displayed in major department stores. At the same time, he acted as a broker for rare treasures. He sold originals and copies of the so-called Romanoff treasures. He also opened the Hammer Galleries in New York to deal in other art that was secretly supplied by the Russian government. Hammer claimed the art was his—that he had accumulated it during his stay in Russia. In reality, it was art supplied from the stash the Russians took during the revolution and stored in warehouses. This was done to bypass US laws that didn't recognize the confiscation of property as a legal transfer of ownership.

By the 1940s, with World War II ending, Armand was living the life of a millionaire in the United States. He was married to his second wife. With her money, he traveled lavishly in his private plane, promoting the Hammer Galleries and the Romanoff treasures. He did this until his wife got tired of his always being away and left him. With his marriage ending, Armand retreated to Florida. There he met Bettye Murphy, who he claimed was the love of his life. Armand promised to marry Bettye as soon as his divorce was final.

When his divorce became final, and Bettye was five months pregnant with his child, Armand had a change of heart. He didn't want to marry Bettye. He wanted to marry Frances Barret, a wealthy widow from Los Angeles. Bettye would have to settle for being his mistress. He set her up in an apartment in Mexico City, where she had his child. Bettye was never to tell their daughter who her father was. In exchange, Hammer agreed to support Bettye for the rest of her life.

Relocated in Los Angeles, Hammer used Frances's money to buy a dying oil company called Occidental Petroleum. It was listed on the New York Stock Exchange. Occidental fortunes had been falling for years because its wells were running dry. Hammer saw it as an opportunity to use Occidental's stock to make acquisitions and raise needed cash. His buying and subsequent promotion of the company sent the stock price up practically overnight. Even though nothing changed, Hammer took advantage of any opportunity to promote the stock.

Three years after Hammer took over Occidental, the company hit the second-largest gas field ever discovered in California. This large strike energized Armand like never before. When he heard that Libya was taking bids from oil companies to drill, he took his plane, OXY ONE, to Libya. Told that Occidental was too small to compete with the major oil companies, Hammer did not give up. Drawing on his money-laundering days and paying bribes to the Russians, he set out to find the right person to help him gain access to the Libyan fields.

He used several groups of contacts before he finally managed to make the necessary payments to the men in power. Thus, when the bids were finally awarded, the "too small to compete" Occidental Petroleum Company beat out the Seven Sisters (which was how the major oil companies were referred to, as they controlled 90 percent of the world's oil supply.)

Occidental was awarded the two prized fields in Libya. They contained an estimated three billion barrels of oil. Overnight, Hammer turned Occidental into a billion-dollar oil company. He had broken the cartel of the Seven Sisters.

Hammer used Occidental money as if it was his personal bank account. Even though he didn't own a controlling share of Occidental, the board of directors was handpicked to give him control. When new directors were elected, Hammer had them sign an undated resignation letter, which Hammer filled in should he need to dismiss a director for not doing his bidding. Hammer also set up trading companies, separate from Occidental, so he could create profits that would be out of the view of stockholders. He used these profits to make payoffs and control the powerful.

Hammer was willing to deal with the enemy when it suited him. For instance, when Omar Gaddafi seized power in Libya, Hammer was in jeopardy of losing his prized oil fields and their enormous profits. What could have been a disaster for Occidental, Hammer turned into a gold mine.

Gaddafi wanted to purge Libya of the corruption that had plagued the country. He wanted Hammer to help him. Gaddafi wanted to know the people Hammer had bribed to get his fields. Given the choice between being prosecuted by the Libyans or giving up his contacts, Hammer chose the latter. Gaddafi also demanded price control of the oil that came from the fields. He wanted a larger share of the revenue.

Using Hammer's Occidental Petroleum as a model, Gaddafi applied the blow that finally broke the back of the oil cartel. He changed the oil business and the lives of the citizens of the world forever.

One by one, each oil-producing Arab country wrested control away from the major oil companies. With that control, the Arab states unified themselves under the Organization of Petroleum Exporting Countries—better known as OPEC. They set prices that rose almost overnight, soaring from one dollar a barrel to thirty-five dollars a barrel. The value of the reserves on Occidental's books rose by billions.

Eventually, Occidental's fields and service contracts were nationalized by the Libyans. It was about then that Occidental discovered a new field. It contained over three billion barrels of reserves deep in the jungles of South America. Hammer's problem was getting the oil out from the well to distribution centers.

Rebels controlled the jungle where Hammer's men were working on a 240-mile pipeline. The pipeline workers were constantly shot at and in danger of their lives. Hammer went to South America to find a solution. Going against the wishes of the local government, Hammer hired the rebels to protect his pipeline even though he knew the money he paid would ultimately find its way back to support the rebels against the government. The rebels worked as security officers, caterers, and drillers. This solved Hammer's problems.

Hammer lived his life up close and personal to power. Occidental money—and the money he siphoned off for his slush fund—was used to put him in the company of powerful people. Donations in the hundreds of thousands of dollars were pledged to politicians and heads of state. If Hammer was ever ignored, he increased the donations for "pay for favors" to see to it that someone did his bidding. If he had to, Hammer committed Occidental to partake in unprofitable projects to obtain an audience with the powerful elite. These nonprofit projects cost Occidental over $2.5 billion. They were shut down after Hammer's death.

Richard Nixon's presidency reopened a door for Hammer. It was Nixon who called for better relations with Russia. He lifted the embargo that was hurting Hammer's trade with the Soviet Union. Nixon and his secretary of state, Henry Kissinger, promoted what was known as détente. This was a policy aimed at improving relations and trade with the Soviet Union.

Hammer's relationship with Nixon was the only time that Nixon saw himself as being on the other side of the law. Not that there weren't attempts or investigations to put him there. Something as trivial as an illegal campaign, and his subsequent attempt to hide that fact, put a stain on his reputation in what he saw as an otherwise impeccable career.

With the resignation of Richard Nixon and the preoccupation of the country with Watergate, détente took a back seat. Hammer was hopeful it would be put on track when a new Republican candidate emerged. This turned out to be Ronald Reagan. But when Hammer heard Reagan speak at a rally where he referred to the Russian government as "the Evil Empire," Hammer knew that a Reagan administration would not renew talks. It would be up to Hammer to continue the dialogue.

With well-placed donations and bribes, Hammer managed to get an invitation to the White House. Reagan knew that Hammer was Russia's man and ignored him. Not to be deterred, Hammer set out to become Reagan's friend by befriending Nancy Reagan. Hammer also donated over $1 million to redecorate the White House. This, as well as his close relationship with the Russian government and its new chief, Mikhail Gorbachev, positioned Hammer as the perfect broker for the Reagan/Gorbachev Summit.

Hammer then set his sights on winning a Nobel Peace Prize. Hammer's belief that he worked his whole life to broker and sponsor peace convinced him that he was the perfect candidate. Never mind that a business leader had never been awarded the

Nobel Peace Prize in its eighty-year history. This might have been easy to get around, but his misdemeanor conviction on the illegal donation to Nixon made him ineligible to be nominated for the prize. Somehow, Hammer needed to expunge the conviction. He needed to get a presidential pardon.

To persuade Reagan to pardon him, Hammer pledged to donate over $1 million to the Reagan Library. When the pardon didn't happen, Hammer increased his pledge to $1.6 million. At the end of his term, Reagan handed out thirty-six presidential pardons. None of them were for Hammer.

Armand Hammer eventually got his pardon from George H. W. Bush. The Reagan Library never received the $1.6 million.

Hammer needed someone to nominate him for the Nobel Peace Prize. He cultivated many possibilities, spending millions of dollars in cash donations aimed at his targeted causes. Prince Charles seemed the most likely to nominate Hammer. To win Charles's favor, Hammer spent millions on the prince's favorite charities. Hammer gave millions to build an American campus for Charles's United World College. When the Armand Hammer United World College opened in 1982, Hammer was sure he would get the nod. But it didn't come from Charles. It came from Menachem Begin, the former prime minister of Israel, who had himself been awarded the prize.

Hammer never did win the Nobel Peace Prize. He did, however, secure many other honors during the course of his lifetime. He received more than thirty honorary degrees and awards. They included the Soviet Union's "Lenin Friendship of the People" medal, an award that had never been given to a foreigner; the American National Medal of Arts; France's Legion of Honor; Italy's Grand Order of Merit; Sweden's Royal Order of the Polar Star; Austria's Knight Commander's Cross; Pakistan's Hilal-i-Quaid-Azam Peace Award; Israel's Leadership Award; Venezuela's Order of Andrés Bello; Mexico's National Recognition Award; Bulgaria's Jubilee Medal; and Belgium's Order of the Crown.

When Hammer reached his seventies, he wanted to cement his name in history. To achieve that goal, Hammer began to collect fine art. He acquired a pristine collection, not the fake and inferior pieces he'd peddled for the Soviets in his Hammer Gallery. He wanted the greatest private art collection ever assembled to be displayed in perpetuity in an Armand Hammer museum. Hammer hired some of the most renowned art authorities and spared no expense in using Occidental's money to acquire the very best.

Hammer's plan was to have the Los Angeles Museum of Art build a wing with his name on it, in three-foot letters, to house his collection. When the museum wouldn't commit to a new wing, he had Occidental pay for a building of its own which would be named the Armand Hammer Museum. It was located next to the company's headquarters. Armand's name was indeed displayed in three-foot letters. Turns out that Occidental paid for more than the building. The company's money was used to send the collection on tour around the world under the Hammer name before it reached its permanent home at the Armand Hammer Museum. Hammer convinced the board that promoting Armand Hammer was synonymous with promoting Occidental. After all, the Occidental reputation and success were a result of Hammer's diplomacy.

That is not how things turned out. After Hammer died at the age of ninety-two, the executives eradicated the memory of Armand Hammer. His name came off halls, lobbies, and conference rooms. His massive portrait in the lobby of the company headquarters was taken down. Occidental's financial annual report gave little mention of his passing. It only included a small picture of him in memoriam. The Armand Hammer Museum and art collection was given to the University of California, Los Angeles. The school sold part of the collection and changed the direction of the exhibit hall to include other works of art. The collections were intermingled with other parts of the college, though the three-foot letters did remain on the outside façade of the building.

Hammer's legacy was further diminished when only a small group of people showed up for his funeral. None of the recipients of bribes and donations, those who Hammer "bought" over the years, attended. He wasn't there to pay them off. Two of his mistresses were at the funeral, along with Victoria, the daughter he refused to acknowledge. His son and grandchildren were there. But each had been written out of his will so that Hammer could spend his money on what he perceived as immortality.

So what happened to the Hammer fortune? Turns out, it wasn't much. Hammer left an estate valued at a mere $40 million. Yes, a large sum of money, but not what one would expect for a man of Hammer's stature.

What happened to the $40 million? Shortly after the will was read, the estate was sued by many of the organizations to which Hammer had made pledges. The Reagan Library sued for its $1.6 million. The Metropolitan Museum in New York sued for its $2 million pledge, which went unpaid; the Met settled for $1 million and removed the Hammer name from a pavilion in the museum. There were other lawsuits, too, from mistresses, employees, entertainers, and his dead wife's estate. The Hammer name lived on in the courts.

When Hammer died in 1990, Occidental's stock was trading at around ten dollars a share. During the years that Hammer controlled the company, the stock rarely traded over twenty dollars a share. Ten years after Hammer passed away, Occidental's management was in full control of the company. They were independent of Hammer's influence and "diplomacy." It was then that the Occidental stock hit one hundred dollars per share. It did so without the man who believed that he *was* Occidental. The stock continues to fluctuate at that price point today.

OCCIDENTAL PETROLEUM CORPORATION
10889 WILSHIRE BOULEVARD · SUITE 1500
LOS ANGELES, CALIFORNIA 90024
(213) 208-8800

ARMAND HAMMER
CHAIRMAN AND
CHIEF EXECUTIVE OFFICER

September 30, 1988

Mr. Sam Shelton
505 Broad Street
Mount Airy, North Carolina 27030

Dear Mr. Shelton:

I wish to thank you for your letter of September 17th and
to let you know that I appreciate your taking the time to write
with such supportive remarks about my career.

With best wishes,

Sincerely,

Armand Hammer

AH:cmj

Document signed by Armand hammer on his personal
stationary. Although his name has been associated with
the baking soda his name actually came from the Russian
revolution symbol of the hammer and sickle. Hammers father
was a leader in the American Communist Party.

Acknowledgments

I would like to acknowledge the authors who have done remarkable and detailed research for their own published works. I have used these biographies, corporate histories, and newspaper and magazine articles as reference material. The following is a list of books that I have read, enjoyed, and recommend if you are interested in learning more about the subjects contained in these pages.

The Billionaire Who Wasn't: How Chuck Feeney Made and Gave Away a Fortune Without Anyone Knowing by Conor O'Clery

Sweet and Low: A Family Story by Rich Cohen

The House of Morgan: An American Banking Dynasty and the Rise of Modern Finance by Ron Chernow

Titan: The Life of John D. Rockefeller, Sr. by Ron Chernow

The Match King: Ivar Kreuger, the Financial Genius Behind a Century of Wall Street Scandals by Frank Partnoy

Crosley: Two Brothers and a Business Empire That Transformed the Nation by Rusty McClure, David Stern, and Michael A. Banks

The Emperors of Chocolate: Inside the Secret World of Hershey and Mars by Joël Glenn Brenner

Dossier: The Secret History of Armand Hammer by Edward Jay Epstein

The People's Tycoon: Henry Ford and the American Century by Steven Watts

The Associates: Four Capitalists Who Created California by Richard Rayner

Fallen Founder: The Life of Aaron Burr by Nancy Isenberg

In-N-Out Burger: A Behind-the-Counter Look at the Fast-Food Chain That Breaks All the Rules by Stacey Perman

A. P. Giannini: Banker of America by Felice A. Bonadio

Secret Formula: How Brilliant Marketing and Relentless Salesmanship Made Coca-Cola the Best-Known Product in the World by Frederick L. Allen

Insull: The Rise and Fall of a Billionaire Utility Tycoon by Forrest McDonald

The Deal Maker: How William C. Durant Made General Motors by Axel Madsen

Remembering Woolworth's: A Nostalgic History of the World's Most Famous Five-and-Dime by Karen Plunkett-Powell

They Made America by Harold Evans, Gail Buckland, and David Lefer

Forbes Greatest Business Stories of All Time by Daniel Gross

Ringlingville USA: The Stupendous Story of Seven Siblings and Their Stunning Circus Success by Jerry Apps

The Invisible Billionaire: Daniel Ludwig by Jerry Shields